Jean Paul Marat

**Revolutionary Lives**

Series Editors: Brian Doherty, Keele University; Sarah Irving, University of Edinburgh; and Professor Paul Le Blanc, La Roche College, Pittsburgh

*Revolutionary Lives* is a book series of short introductory critical biographies of radical political figures. The books are sympathetic but not sycophantic, and the intention is to present a balanced and where necessary critical evaluation of the individual's place in their political field, putting their actions and achievements in context and exploring issues raised by their lives, such as the use or rejection of violence, nationalism, or gender in political activism. While individuals are the subject of the books, their personal lives are dealt with lightly except in so far as they mesh with political issues. The focus of these books is the contribution their subjects have made to history, an examination of how far they achieved their aims in improving the lives of the oppressed and exploited, and how they can continue to be an inspiration for many today.

**Published titles:**

*Leila Khaled: Icon of Palestinian Liberation*
Sarah Irving

*Jean Paul Marat: Tribune of the French Revolution*
Clifford D. Conner

*Gerrard Winstanley: The Digger's Life and Legacy*
John Gurney

www.revolutionarylives.co.uk

# Jean Paul Marat

## Tribune of the French Revolution

Clifford D. Conner

**Pluto**Press
www.plutobooks.com

First published 2012 by Pluto Press
345 Archway Road, London N6 5AA

www.plutobooks.com

Distributed in the United States of America exclusively by
Palgrave Macmillan, a division of St. Martin's Press LLC,
175 Fifth Avenue, New York, NY 10010

British Library Cataloguing in Publication Data
A catalogue record for this book is available from the British Library

ISBN   978 0 7453 3194 2   Hardback
ISBN   978 0 7453 3193 5   Paperback
ISBN   978 1 84964 679 6   PDF
ISBN   978 1 84964 681 9   Kindle
ISBN   978 1 84964 680 2   ePub

Library of Congress Cataloging in Publication Data applied for

This book is printed on paper suitable for recycling and made from fully
managed and sustained forest sources. Logging, pulping and manufacturing
processes are expected to conform to the environmental standards of the
country of origin.

10   9   8   7   6   5   4   3   2   1

Designed and produced for Pluto Press by Chase Publishing Services Ltd
Typeset from disk by Stanford DTP Services, Northampton, England
Simultaneously printed digitally by CPI Antony Rowe, Chippenham, UK and
Edwards Bros in the United States of America

*To three American prisoners of conscience*

Lynne Stewart
Mumia Abu-Jamal
Bradley Manning

*To learn more about these courageous victims of injustice, go to*

www.MaratScience.com

and click on "Dedication"

# Contents

# List of Illustrations

# Preface

I have long been wary of authors who claim to have discovered some startlingly important aspect of history that all previous authors had somehow overlooked. Now I find myself reluctantly having to make a claim almost (but not quite) like that.

Jean Paul Marat was a key leader of what was arguably the most important of all social revolutions. And yet there have been virtually no adequate biographies of Marat published in the English language. Why not?

I am hard pressed to answer that question. The reason that I am not claiming to be the *only* adequate biographer of Marat is contained in the qualifying phrase "in the English language." Numerous fine biographies have appeared in French—my personal favorites are Jean Massin's and Olivier Coquard's[1]— but none have been published in English translation. The present volume is intended to remedy that glaring omission in the literature on the French Revolution.

As for previous English-language biographies of Marat, there have been a grand total of *two* published in the past hundred years. One was by the distinguished historian Louis Gottschalk and the other was by me.[2] Gottschalk's, which was originally published in 1927 and reissued, unchanged, in 1967, is not simply out of date, but in my opinion is also seriously flawed in its interpretation of Marat's role in the Revolution.

Gottschalk portrayed Marat as an accidental figure on the stage of history—an ultraradical demagogue who gained immense notoriety but should not be counted among the authentic leaders of the Revolution. In 1997 I published a biography of Marat to challenge that notion. *Au contraire*, I argued, Marat was a highly effective leader of the French Revolution who earned his influence through the consistency and principled nature of his leadership.

My 1997 biography of Marat is not out of date, but I felt it would now be useful to write another one with a different focus.

Although the earlier book did not ignore Marat's revolutionary activity, it put more emphasis on his much longer career as a scientist. That was an aspect of his life that had not previously been treated adequately even by French biographers.

The volume you now hold in your hands, however, centers its attention squarely on Marat's political career as journalist, agitator, and leader of the French Revolution during the last four years of his life, 1789–93. That, after all, is the basis of his historical importance and what he is rightfully remembered for. Without Marat, the French Revolution may well not have resulted in the social transformation of France, Europe, and the world.

Marat's pre-Revolutionary careers as a medical doctor and an experimental physicist are not irrelevant to his later development, however. To fully come to grips with this enigmatic figure, it is necessary to take that formative part of his life into account. For that reason, I have created a website devoted primarily to an exposition of Marat's medical and scientific work during the years 1765 through 1789, which I invite readers of this volume to peruse (www.MaratScience.com).

*     *     *

The French Revolution dealt the death blow to the traditional social structure not only in France but throughout Europe. The old regime had been founded on the principle of natural inequality: that some people were by birth superior to others and thereby entitled to special privileges. The Revolution produced a social order based on the opposite premise of human equality, from which derived the rights to equality before the law, representative government, and guarantees of civil liberties.

But to Marat these gains, however important, did not go nearly far enough. They amounted to a great leap forward in *political* equality but not *economic* equality. The rich and poor gained equal rights to sleep under the bridges of Paris, but the wretched of the earth remained mired in their wretchedness. What set Marat apart from all other major figures of the Revolution—from Mirabeau to Brissot to Danton to Robespierre—was his total identification with the struggle of the propertyless classes for full social equality.

The ever-deepening gulf between the billionaires and the slumdogs in today's world testifies to the continuing relevance of Marat's revolutionary perspective. Properly understood, the triumphs and failures of his career shed light on some timeless and universal aspects of the revolutionary process that can benefit—and perhaps inspire—participants in the current struggles for social change. May they triumph, and the sooner the better.

*Clifford D. Conner*
*November 2011*

# Acknowledgment

This book owes its existence first of all to Paul Le Blanc and the debt is twofold. It was he who in 1997 originally asked me, on behalf of what at that time was Humanities Press, to write a biography of Marat, which I did. And then it was also he who more recently asked me, on behalf of Pluto Press, to write the biography of Marat you are presently holding in your hand. Thank you twice, Paul.

# List of Abbreviations

| | |
|---|---|
| Actes | *Actes de la Commune de Paris pendant la Révolution* (Paris, 1894–1914) |
| AP | *Ami du peuple* (September 1789–September 1792) |
| Arch. Parl. | *Archives Parlementaires de 1787 à 1860* (Paris, 1867 et seq.) |
| Correspondance | *La Correspondance de Marat*, C. Vellay, ed. (Paris: Charpentier et Fasquelle, 1908) |
| JRF | *Journal de la République Française* (September 1792–March 1793) |
| MHdS | *Marat homme de science?*, J. F. Lemaire and J. P. Poirier, eds. (Paris: Synthélabo, 1993) |
| Mon. univ. | *Gazette nationale; ou, le Moniteur universel* (Paris, 1789 et seq.) |
| Œuvres | *Œuvres de Marat*, A. Vermorel, ed. (Paris, Décembre-Alonnier, 1869) |
| Pamphlets | *Les Pamphlets de Marat*, C. Vellay, ed. (Paris: Charpentier et Fasquelle, 1911) |
| PRF | *Publiciste de la République Française* (March 1793–July 1793) |
| Rév. France/Brabant | *Révolutions de France et de Brabant* (Paris, November 1789–July 1792) |
| Soc. Jac. | *La Société des Jacobins: Recueil de documents*, A. Aulard, ed. (Paris, 1889–97) |

Bibliographical Note: The sources are given in the notes. For a comprehensive bibliography, go to www.MaratScience.com and click on "Bibliography."

# Introduction
## The Phantom and the Historians

The French Revolution divided France and eventually all of Europe with a line of blood. The loyalties and hatreds to which it gave birth have endured to the present day. Jean Paul Marat, more than any other individual, has for over two centuries remained the focus of the passionate emotions unleashed by that great social upheaval.

Marat's celebrity derived first of all from his role as the most influential of the Revolution's journalists and agitators. Of the hundreds of competing journals that appeared when censorship collapsed at the onset of the Revolution, it was his *Ami du peuple*—The People's Friend—that most thoroughly expressed the aspirations and focused the fury of the Parisian poor.

Many decades later Victor Hugo recognized Marat as a timeless symbol of social revolution. "As long as there are *misérables*," wrote the author of *Les Misérables*, "there will be a cloud on the horizon that can become a phantom and a phantom that can become Marat."[1] Fear of this powerful phantom, and of its reappearance, has made a dispassionate evaluation of the historic Marat all but impossible. It has led innumerable authors to consciously or subconsciously distort their portrayals of him. In general, conservative and liberal historians alike have detested Marat; the conservatives because he was a threat to the status quo, and the liberals because of the extremism and calls to violence that characterized his agitational style.

In the 1950s, with the Cold War at its peak, a group of British and American historians issued a "revisionist" challenge to the Marxist interpretation that had dominated the study of the French Revolution during the first half of the twentieth century. Their primary target was Georges Lefebvre's masterful synthesis that had become the standard account of the Revolution.[2]

Jean Paul Marat. After Marat's death his sister Albertine said that of all the portraits of her brother, this one looked most like him. ("Marat en 1793" by Joseph Boze, Carnavalet Museum, Paris)

The revisionist history downplayed the Revolution's significance as a cause of social change and denied that its most radical phase from September 1793 through July 1794 contributed anything of value to future generations. From this it followed that Marat's role in the Revolution was likewise of little value. The present biography reflects the more traditional view, held by Marxists and non-Marxists alike, that the French Revolution was a watershed event in the development of modern society, and seeks to establish that Marat's historic contribution to it was indispensable.

The historians' fear and loathing of the revolutionary phantom has led them to portray Marat as a villain with no redeeming qualities. According to their collective portrait, his character was that of a common criminal. He was a psychopath, a sociopath, a quack, and a charlatan. Even his physical appearance was repulsive.

Consistency has not been the strong suit of Marat's critics, however. The descriptions portraying him as horribly ugly do not square with the charge against his character that he frequently seduced the beautiful wives of his friends and patrons. One author, for example, depicted Marat as a "sallow man with pockpitted countenance, black flat hair, blood-shotten blinking eyes and spasmodically twitching mouth—the incarnation of the repulsive," while also alleging that he seduced the famous artist Angelica Kauffmann and the Marquise de l'Aubespine.[3]

The frequent claims that Marat was a criminal, a psychopath, and a charlatan are obviously more important than whether he was ugly or not. Each of these allegations merits particular consideration.

## WAS MARAT A COMMON CRIMINAL?

The meager material conditions in which Marat lived when his political influence was at its peak support his claim to have been, like Robespierre, incorruptible. A number of important historians, however, accepted as true, or at least plausible, a long-standing rumor that Marat had committed a museum robbery in England in 1776. British historian Sidney L. Phipson analyzed the supporting evidence at book length and concluded that Marat had indeed been a common thief. Phipson claimed that he had examined the charges against Marat very carefully and had presented the evidence "without, at least, any conscious bias."[4]

To Phipson the moral lesson of this felonious deed was very clear:

> Jean Paul Marat was by no means the irreproachable figure he is so often depicted, but belongs, rather … to that more questionable class of politicians who qualified for revolutionary triumphs by early infractions

of the criminal law. But nations have never been saved, although thrones may be overturned, by patriots of this stamp.[5]

The essence of Phipson's case was that Marat, using the alias "Jean Pierre Le Maître," stole some rare coins from an Oxford University museum, was caught and sentenced to prison, but escaped and fled to France. The occurrence of the museum theft is undisputed; at issue is whether Le Maître was in fact Marat. A circumstance that Phipson felt could not be coincidental was that Le Maître was also known to have used the name "Mara," and Marat's original family name had been "Mara."

The claim that they were one and the same person originated in an English publication in 1793 and was thereafter buttressed by "eyewitness testimony," which Phipson evaluated and deemed probably true. By systematically accepting all of the rumor material and rejecting all conflicting evidence, he produced a believable narrative leading to the conclusion that Marat was the coin thief.

The main obstacle that Phipson faced in pleading this case was the fact that Marat was undeniably back in France, and in respectable circumstances, just three months after Le Maître had been sentenced to five years hard labor in England. One month after Le Maître's conviction, however, six convicts broke out of the prison and escaped. The names of the escapees are not known, but Phipson's case depends on his assumption that Le Maître was one of the six.[6]

The most significant piece of counterevidence that Phipson considered but rejected was a letter written by Marat datelined "Douvres, 11 avril 1776," in which he says he is leaving England.[7] That date falls between February 1776, when Le Maître was arrested, and March 1777, when he was on trial. Phipson conceded that Le Maître was in prison at that time, but he speculated that Marat deliberately wrote the letter after the fact to cover up his criminal past. There is no evidence, however, that Marat was ever aware of being suspected of any robbery.

Phipson's case is based entirely on circumstantial evidence. It depends upon a long chain of implicit links to Marat that he judges to be "probable" or "not impossible." Nonetheless, it was deemed to be at least plausible by other historians who, like Phipson, perhaps felt a need to believe the worst about Marat.[8]

Fortunately this issue was put to rest in 1966 when Robert Darnton discovered a document in the archives of the Société Typographique de Neuchâtel. It was a letter from Marat to F. S. Ostervald, one of the Société's founders.[9] The letter is dated May 14, 1776, and proves that Marat was then in Geneva. It can therefore now be said without a doubt that Marat did not rob the museum. The episode reveals nothing about Marat, but a great deal about how historians allow their social prejudices to affect their judgment.

## WAS MARAT CLINICALLY INSANE?

To readers today, Marat's political polemics often appear harsh and unduly violent. But that is largely because they are usually presented apart from their political context—namely, Paris in the throes of rebellion from 1789 to 1793. His writings appear less "extremist" in nature when the extreme circumstances in which he was operating are taken into account.

When a bitter opponent of the Revolution such as Hippolyte Taine portrayed Marat as a violence-obsessed madman, his greater purpose was to condemn by proxy the demands and aspirations of plebeian Parisians—which he called "the mob"— as irrational and insane. A more recent author offered this typical appraisal: "Jean Paul Marat was a fanatic; he was sincere; he was violent and bloodthirsty; he was enthusiastically and lyrically devoted to the Revolution; and he was probably insane."[10]

Marat may well have been eccentric, moody, difficult to get along with, or suspicious by nature, but that is not the issue. Is there any evidence that he was a certifiable psychopath? A prominent American neurologist and psychologist, Charles W. Burr, M.D., advanced the claim that Marat's deeds and writings prove he was psychotic and clinically insane.[11] Burr's 1919 article has frequently been cited by later authors.[12] It is difficult to

understand how the historians who have echoed his opinion
could have missed the blatant class bias that underpinned his
psychoanalysis of Marat. Marat's "creed was simple—all that
the rich own belongs to the poor because they stole it from the
poor," Burr wrote. "He belongs then among the insane, and is
an example of paranoia of the political type."[13]

Dr. Burr wrote this article two years after the triumph of the
Russian Revolution, in which he must have perceived Marat's
phantom. The political component of his definition of insanity
is undisguised:

> The gentlemen who regard [Marat] as a political genius, e.g., the sincere
> members of the Bolshevik party of today, not only in this country, are
> themselves mentally abnormal. He is not the only lunatic in history who
> has had a following during life and after death.[14]

Burr's diagnosis of Marat's mental problems reveals that
his own social fears extended from communism to feminism,
reflected the generation gap that alienated youth from their
parents, and included an element of xenophobia:

> Mentally, in his earlier life in many ways he resembled the sentimental
> sympathizers with Bolshevism who are today making so much noise in
> America. It is noteworthy that almost all the Americans born among them
> have led shielded lives, have never been in contact with the realities of
> life, have never had to work (their fathers did that for them); the women
> advocates have failed in woman's first and natural function. Among
> the foreign born are internationalists, parasites, and those who left the
> countries of their birth for their countries' good.[15]

Burr's analysis goes beyond bias to bigotry and serves as an
extreme example of the fatuity of seeking a scientific basis for
judging a revolutionary leader insane. Marat and the Parisian
poor whose mental state he reflected were not crazy; they
were angry, and their anger was not at all irrational. Marat's
psychological health is impossible to evaluate with precision,
but there is no indication that he crossed the line into psychosis.

Historians have pointed to Marat's frequent allegations of plots against his life as evidence of paranoia. Whether or not his suspicions and accusations were exaggerated, they were certainly not totally unfounded. His perception of being persecuted by his political enemies was not imaginary. He was repeatedly arrested, hounded into hiding and exile, and ultimately assassinated.

## WAS MARAT A CHARLATAN?

For more than two centuries the general attitude of historians toward Marat's medical and scientific practice has been unrelentingly hostile. L. F. Maury's interpretation is typical: "Marat, that charlatan, that bloodthirsty fool, who threw himself into revolutionary excesses out of an insensate pride and a hatred of his betters, imagined himself to be a physicist capable of dethroning Newton."[16]

Some recent studies have offered a more objective reassessment of Marat's scientific work. The traditional view that dismissed it as charlatanism or pseudoscience, however, was part of the larger ideological campaign against the revolutionary phantom. If Marat's scientific ideas were simply fraudulent, why should anything more be expected of his political ideas? On the other hand, if Marat were to be recognized as a legitimate scientist, that would give him credit for at least some degree of intellectual prowess. And if that were the case, then his rise to prominence during the Revolution could not be written off as a mere accident of history, as his detractors have maintained.

Marat's critics have repeatedly depicted his scientific activities and ideas as unimpressive at best and ridiculous at worst. But to make their case, they have had to take them out of their eighteenth-century context and measure them against the criteria of twentieth- or twenty-first-century science. Small wonder that on that scale Marat has failed to measure up as a scientist. The only legitimate way to assess any scientist's accomplishments is to evaluate them in the context of the science of his or her contemporaries.

By that standard, Marat was in no sense a charlatan or a quack. His scientific practice was fully legitimate in the sense in which science was understood in the 1780s. Marat was not on the "fringes" of science in the eyes of his contemporaries, but was at the heart of it. It could be argued that he was on the fringes of the *elite* science establishment, as represented by the Parisian Academy of Sciences, but that is quite a different matter. Throughout the ages, many important scientific contributions have been made by men and women whom the scientific elite tried to marginalize.[17]

## WAS MARAT A REVOLUTIONARY LEADER?

Establishing that Marat was not a thief, a lunatic, or a quack does not tell us what he *was*, and why his life was historically important. All historians acknowledge that he was a revolutionary, and none would deny that he attained a great deal of popularity. Beyond those two points, however, agreement is rare. Some have argued that Marat's revolutionary role was more image than substance—all sound and fury, signifying nothing.[18]

The central theme of this biography is that Marat was not simply an icon of radicalism or a notorious demagogue, but one of the authentic leaders whose presence was crucial to the success of the French Revolution. Chapters 1 and 2 present a brief account of Marat's life prior to the pivotal insurrection at the Bastille in 1789, and Chapters 3 through 5 offer a narrative of Marat's activities from 1789 to the end of his life. A conscientious examination of those activities demonstrates that he was not an opportunist devoted primarily to advancing his own interests, but a principled leader continuously seeking to advance the Revolution.

# 1
## The Early Years

Jean Paul Marat, renowned as the staunchest of French patriots, was not originally a Frenchman at all. In fact, he did not even begin life as a Marat. His name at birth was Jean Paul Mara; he added the "t" to his surname later, after he moved to France. Some hostile commentators have depicted this as an indication of Marat's duplicity, but it had no moral significance. It was not uncommon for people in eighteenth-century France to alter the spelling of their names.

Marat was born on May 24, 1743, not in France and not of French parents. His birthplace was Boudry, a town in the principality of Neuchâtel, which is now in Switzerland. At that time, however, Neuchâtel was a possession of the Prussian King, Frederick the Great. His father, Jean Mara, was born in Caglieri, Sardinia, in 1703; his first languages were Spanish and Italian. In 1740 Jean Mara moved to Geneva and married sixteen-year-old Louise Cabrol, a native of Geneva who was descended from French Huguenots. Jean Paul was the first of the Maras' six children. Although his primary language was French, contemporaries report that even in adulthood he spoke French with a somewhat foreign-sounding accent.[1] The first two of Marat's siblings, Henri and Marie, were born in 1745 and 1746. Then, after a ten-year hiatus, David was born in 1756, Albertine in 1760, and Jean Pierre in 1767.[2]

The Maras were city-dwellers of modest means; the head of the household was well educated but did not have a stable profession. There are indications, however, that their social status improved over time. When Jean Paul was baptized in 1743 he had no godfather, suggesting that the family was socially isolated, whereas the three younger children born between 1756 and 1767 all had godparents, some of whom were substantial citizens. At the age of 16, Jean Paul left home to seek his fortune. Authors anxious to portray him in a bad light have speculated that his father banished him from the family home, but again there is no evidence to support that claim. On the contrary, by all accounts his relations with his family were excellent. In 1776 he returned home for a visit, about which he wrote, "I couldn't deny myself the pleasure of spending some time with my folks."[3] After Marat's assassination, three of his siblings publicly proclaimed their appreciation to Simonne Évrard, his widow, for her devotion to their brother.[4]

Marat's mother and father died in 1782 and 1783, respectively. Shortly before his own death, Marat wrote very warmly of them. He credited his mother with developing his social conscience, and his father with instilling a love of learning in him. An autobiographical sketch that he published in 1793 said that he felt "exceptionally fortunate to have had the advantage of receiving a very careful education in my paternal home. I was able to avoid all the nasty habits of childhood that overstimulate and degrade a man."[5] In addition to wanting posterity to know that as a boy he had abstained from masturbation, he also stressed his rectitude in sexual matters in general: "I was able to avoid the temptations of adolescence and reached manhood without ever giving in to tempestuous passions. I was still a virgin at the age of 21 and had long since devoted myself to studious meditation."

Although Marat's outlook evidently included a strong puritanical streak, the main reason he alluded to his sexual abstinence was to emphasize how deeply serious he had been even as a child. But more important to his future evolution into a tribune of revolution was the abhorrence of oppression and injustice that his mother had imparted to him early on: "I had already developed a sense of morality by the time I was eight years old. At that age, I couldn't bear to see other people treated badly; the sight of cruelty filled me with anger and witnessing an injustice made my heart race as if I myself were the victim."

## LEAVING THE NEST

When the teenaged Marat left home he headed for France to seek an education. His precise path is uncertain, but it seems that after brief stays in Toulouse and Montpellier he was attracted to Bordeaux, an intellectual center that had been home to Montesquieu, whom Marat later claimed as a primary intellectual influence. He settled there, attending classes at the university of Bordeaux and paying for them out of the wages he earned as a tutor.

Bordeaux was a commercial center as well, and Marat was hired to teach the children of one of its leading citizens, Paul Nairac. Nairac was a wealthy ship-owner and sugar merchant whose fortune derived from colonial commerce, including slave trading. In 1786, on the eve of the Revolution, the Nairac family would officially join the aristocratic class, having purchased the necessary credentials. Marat's association with the Nairacs most likely allowed him to meet powerful people who would later be instrumental in advancing his career.

The young man was apparently too restless to remain in the provinces for long, however, so after only two years in Bordeaux, in 1762 he did what any ambitious youth with dreams of glory would do—he left for Paris. Marat's activities during his first stay in Paris are not recorded, but he seems to have pursued his education in an informal way that was typical of the era. Rather than enrolling in a particular institution and pursuing a specific diploma, he attended classes in various places and read voraciously. The curriculum he set for himself included medicine, physics, philosophy, politics, and literature.

It may have been during these early days in Paris that Marat first attempted to become a writer. He produced a 600-page manuscript of a romantic historical novel set during a Polish civil war, *The Adventures of the Young Count Potowski*. If he attempted to publish it, he did not succeed, but he kept the manuscript and more than a half century after his death it was published as a curiosity.[6]

A statement he made later provides some insight into the course of his early intellectual development. "I had hardly reached the age of 18," he wrote, "when the so-called *philosophes* made various attempts to attract me to their party."[7] The philosophers of the French Enlightenment were divided into rival camps. On one side was the central current represented by Voltaire, Diderot, and D'Alembert, and on the other was the countercurrent represented by Jean-Jacques Rousseau. The young Marat was drawn toward Rousseau's "party." Rousseau's radical critique of science and society appealed to Marat no less than it did to an entire generation of young rebels.

After only three years in Paris, however, Marat had apparently had his fill of the metropolis. In order to "avoid the dangers of dissipation," he says, in 1765 he left Paris, moved to England, and became an author. His first work "was aimed at combating materialism,"[8] by which he meant a sterile form of rationalism that he associated with Voltaire and with Newtonianism. His *Essay on the Human Soul* was a monograph of about a hundred pages, written in English, which was published in 1772. The following year he expanded it to two volumes and republished it as *A Philosophical Essay on Man*. Then in 1775 it appeared as *De l'homme*, an even larger French edition published in three volumes by Marc Michel Rey in Amsterdam. Rey, as a major publisher of Rousseau's works, was among the most influential figures of the Enlightenment. Marat had made his debut in the major leagues, so to speak, of French intellectual life.

The neophyte had launched himself into the factional literary politics of the Enlightenment. He must have been thrilled when *De l'homme* provoked a caustic rejoinder from Voltaire[9] and a milder criticism from Diderot.[10] Many years later, during the Revolution, Marat remarked that being the target of Voltaire's sarcasm had put him in good company, because Voltaire "had taken the same liberty with Montesquieu and Rousseau."[11]


## ELEVEN YEARS ABROAD

Following his departure for England in 1765, Marat would remain abroad for eleven years. He was based in London for most of those years, but also spent time in Edinburgh, lived in

Dublin for a year, and then in Holland for another year before returning to Paris in 1776.[12]

In London, Marat set up a medical practice, and by all indications had soon become a moderately successful professional. He was attracted to the London café scene, where he was befriended by a group of talented artists, including Angelica Kauffmann, later a renowned painter, with whom Marat is alleged to have had an amorous liaison. The evidence supporting that allegation, however, is not compelling.[13]

Marat's new circle of acquaintances was primarily composed of foreigners like himself. He seems to have spoken Italian rather than French with a number of them, including Antonio Zucchi, a Venetian artist; Joseph Bonomi, an architect; and Kauffmann, who was not Italian but had lived in Italy for many years.

After writing his *Philosophical Essay on Man*, he sought out prominent scholars and other influential people to seek their support in promoting it. He found at least three who were willing to write testimonials praising the work: Charles Collignon, a professor of physiology at Cambridge University; a French diplomat named La Rochette; and Lord George Lyttleton.[14] Lyttleton also offered to introduce Marat to other important people. A further sign of Marat's rising social status in London was his induction into a Masonic lodge in the fashionable Soho district on July 15, 1774.

From at least October 1774 through February 1775 Marat was in Holland, most likely for the purpose of promoting *Philosophical Essay on Man*. It was during that time that he met Marc Michel Rey and arranged for the publication of the French version. But Marat may have had an additional motive for absenting himself from England. His first political book, *Chains of Slavery*, had just been published in London and its dissident views may have attracted some unwelcome attention from the police.

## MARAT'S *CHAINS OF SLAVERY*

The earliest exposition of Marat's political thought, *Chains of Slavery*, testifies to the fundamental consistency of his outlook over the final 20 years of his life. It reveals a strong element of continuity between the dapper young London medical practitioner and the People's Friend of revolutionary France.

*Chains of Slavery* was inspired by the "Wilkes-and-Liberty" movement in England, a grassroots movement from 1763 to 1774 of partisans of John Wilkes, a popular politician. As an admirer of Montesquieu, Marat had originally admired England as a bastion of freedom in contrast with despotic France. But when he arrived in 1765 he discovered that the grass of English liberties was less green than it had appeared from afar.

Although parliamentary rule had been established for more than a century in England, corruption was widespread and a monarchical party was making a strong effort to recentralize political power in the hands of King George III. In April 1763, Wilkes, a journalist and Member of Parliament, criticized the King. For doing so, he was imprisoned and removed from his seat in the House of Commons. Widespread outrage led to the rapid rise of a boisterous movement demanding Wilkes' reinstatement and freedom of the press. Wilkes did not remain in prison long, but when released he went into exile for four years.

Upon his return to London in 1768, Wilkes ran for parliament and was reelected. Once again, however, he was arrested and his election was invalidated. On May 10, 1768, a demonstration outside the prison where he was being held was fired upon by the government troops, and protestors were killed. Marat later claimed to have been an eyewitness to this event, which is immortalized in British history as "the Massacre of St. George's Fields." Wilkes ran again in the next elections, won a landslide victory, but was again disqualified by the authorities. Then he ran yet again and after another landslide saw the losing candidate declared the winner. In 1774 Wilkes became Lord Mayor of London and was finally allowed to take his seat in the House of Commons. Meanwhile, his often-cheated constituents had become a large and rowdy extra-parliamentary protest movement.

Marat's main contribution to the Wilkes-and-Liberty movement was his *Chains of Slavery*, which appeared in May

1774. It was a verbal assault aimed at tyrannical government in general and at the current British regime of Lord North in particular. The tone of Marat's polemic is evident in its subtitle: "A Work Wherein the Clandestine and Villainous Attempts of Princes to Ruin Liberty Are Pointed out, and the Dreadful Scenes of Despotism Disclosed." Although the book had little impact on the course of English history, it is valuable for what it reveals about Marat's ideological development a decade and a half before the French Revolution.

As with everything concerning Marat, how later commentators have evaluated *Chains of Slavery* has varied widely. In Louis Gottschalk's view, for example, it was an unoriginal book with a few radical passages that are only conspicuous as a result of Marat's later notoriety.[15] Jean Massin, on the other hand, described it as "the first modern treatise on insurrection."[16] *Chains of Slavery* was not entirely original, but it is not surprising that a self-proclaimed disciple of Rousseau would draw upon his master's works.[17] Nevertheless, there were, as Massin pointed out, important aspects of Marat's book that were unprecedented. While Dr. Marat's diagnosis of the degenerative social illnesses he witnessed echoed Rousseau, the therapy he prescribed was considerably more radical. In the book, Marat identified monarchs as the primary oppressors, but also condemned parliaments as their corrupt accomplices. "Who are the friends to the poor," he asked, "in a senate composed of rich men only?"[18]

Marat was certainly not the only author of his era to deplore the extreme gulf separating the wealthy few and the impoverished multitude. Some, such as Mably, Morelly, and Restif de la Bretonne, had proposed very radical communistic solutions. What set Marat apart was his political understanding of the practical measures that would be required to really solve the problems of inequality and despotism. "Liberty," he declared, "constantly springs up out of the fires of sedition."[19] "Has a people ever took arms but to secure their liberty, to oppose the pernicious designs of ambitious men, and to free themselves from oppression?"[20]

Marat did not believe small, violent groups of dedicated revolutionaries could overthrow repressive regimes by their own efforts alone. When the people embark upon an insurrection "their rising avails little, unless it be general."[21] On the other hand, a small cadre of revolutionaries is absolutely necessary to carry out the propaganda and agitational tasks that can organize "the multitude" for insurrectionary action:

> As a continual attention to public affairs is above the reach of the multitude; in a state jealous of its liberty, there should never be wanting some men to watch the transactions of the ministers, unveil their ambitious projects, give an alarm at the approach of the storm, rouse the people from their lethargy, disclose the abyss open before them, and point out those on whom the public indignation ought to fall.[22]

This is a remarkably precise description of how Marat would come to see his own role when confronted with a revolutionary situation in France 15 years later. Several chapters of *Chains of Slavery* provide detailed instructions for agitational journalists, demonstrating a clear continuity between his words of 1774 and his deeds after 1789.

Successful insurrections, Marat insisted, do not occur spontaneously. For an unorganized multitude to be united into a fighting force with the necessary decisiveness, it must subordinate itself to a centralized leadership. Creating that leadership and establishing its authority are the most crucial elements of the art of insurrection.

*Chains of Slavery* appeared in print just a few months before John Wilkes was at last permitted to take his seat in Parliament in late 1774, after which the Wilkes-and-Liberty movement rapidly disbanded. In the context of widespread political complacency, even if Marat's manual of insurrection had been widely known it could not have been put to practical use. The ideas it proposed would remain abstractions until 1789, when an opportunity arose in France to put them to the test.[23]

## RETURNING TO FRANCE

In April 1776, about a year after he returned to England from his sojourn in Holland, Marat took a brief trip to Geneva to visit his parents and then moved back to Paris for good. Although theorizing about insurrections was no more likely to attract a big readership in Paris than in London at that time, Marat did not entirely abandon his political interests. He must have participated with gusto in debating the issues of the day in the Parisian cafés. It was probably then that he and his future political enemy, Jacques Pierre Brissot, became close friends.

Marat spent much of 1777 and 1778 writing a book-length essay for a contest sponsored by the Economic Society of Berne, which had offered a prize for the best detailed proposal for reforming the criminal justice system. Marat's entry, entitled *Plan of Criminal Legislation*, did not win the prize, but it was published at Neuchâtel in 1780, and then Brissot republished it in 1782. In 1790, in the wake of the great uprising that initiated the French Revolution, Marat extensively revised it and had it published again.[24] He judged this to be the "least imperfect" of all his published works.[25]

The *Plan of Criminal Legislation* testified to the empathy with the poor that would later characterize Marat's revolutionary journalism. He argued, for example, that stealing food for survival is not immoral and therefore should not be illegal. The moral content of this sentiment may today seem commonplace, but criminal law in England at that time prescribed death by hanging for theft of property valued at more than one shilling. Grisly public executions designed to strike terror in the hearts of onlookers were common in both England and France.

Marat began his *Plan of Criminal Legislation* with the observation that the existing laws were simply the arbitrary commands of a dominant power structure that served the interests of the few at the expense of the many.[26] Laws against theft, he wrote, are based on the idea of private property, which is also an arbitrary notion: There is no basis in nature for any individual to own a portion of the Earth's surface. "The right to possess," Marat argued,

flows from the right to live. Therefore, all that which is indispensable to our existence belongs to us, and anything more than that cannot legitimately be considered ours as long as others are in need. That is the legitimate basis of property, both in the state of society and in the state of nature.[27]

The *Plan of Criminal Legislation* is the last indication of any interest on Marat's part in political or social affairs before 1789. Whatever passion remained from his involvement with the Wilkes-and-Liberty movement seems to have been sublimated into controversies with medical and scientific institutions. Throughout the decade of political quiescence preceding the Great Revolution, Marat's attention was focused on his careers as physician and physicist.

# 2
# The Physician and the Physicist
## 1765–1789

Marat's first calling was to the art of medicine. He began his medical studies as a teenager in Bordeaux from 1760 to 1762 and continued them in Paris through 1765. It was probably toward the end of that first stay in Paris that Marat cured his first patient. He later wrote of his success in treating a friend afflicted with a case of gleets—a painful and embarrassing manifestation of gonorrheal disease.[1] Shortly thereafter he moved to England, where he practiced medicine for ten or eleven years.

Marat's medical career has often been disparaged by authors who have described him variously as an itinerant quack without credentials, a patent-medicine huckster, or a horse-doctor. In fact, however, he did possess a valid medical degree and achieved professional success as a physician. In England he established his practice on Church Street in Soho, then London's most fashionable section. Later, following his return to Paris in 1776, his clientele consisted of wealthy aristocrats, including high-ranking members of the royal court.

As for Marat's credentials, he was awarded an M.D. degree by St. Andrews University, Scotland, on June 30, 1775.[2] His detractors have claimed that because there is no record of his actually having attended classes there, he must have bought the degree. His diploma was signed, however, by two medical examiners who officially certified Marat's competence as a physician. One of them, Dr. William Buchan, was a prominent medical authority whose books were published in multiple editions in both English and French.[3] Marat's proficiency in the healing arts is further corroborated by two pamphlets he had published that provide detailed accounts of some of his treatments. They testify to his general medical knowledge and to his familiarity with certain specialties, such as eye disease and electrotherapy.[4]

The way St. Andrews bestowed its degrees seems lax according to modern standards of medical education, but such comparisons are anachronistic. When Marat received his M.D. in 1775, he had already been practicing medicine for ten years. It was common in the eighteenth century—and in France even well into the nineteenth—for universities to confer degrees as a way of certifying the professional competence and educational preparation of working practitioners who had not actually attended classes at those institutions. Despite the illustrious Dr. Johnson's famous quip about St. Andrews "growing richer by degrees," the university was not regarded as a mere diploma mill. Benjamin Franklin, for one, expressed pride in the doctorate it had awarded him. Marat's M.D. was unquestionably authentic by the standards of the day.[5]

In 1777, within a year of transferring his practice to Paris, Marat's reputation as a healer received a considerable boost from his success in treating one especially influential patient, the marquise de l'Aubespine. She had long suffered from a chronic respiratory ailment that other doctors had deemed incurable. When she credited Marat with curing her, the case was publicized in the *Gazette de Santé* and Marat's career as a high-society doctor was assured.[6] The marquise was the niece of the duc de Choiseul, one of the King's most powerful ministers, which likely accounts for how Marat gained entrée to the royal court.

From 1777 to 1783 Marat served as a physician in the household of the comte d'Artois, one of King Louis XVI's brothers. It was a prestigious official position that gave him an annual stipend of 2,000 livres in addition to the income from his lucrative private practice. Ironically, Marat's royal patron would later become one of the French Revolution's most fervent enemies, heading an émigré army that would attempt to crush it. After the Bourbon Restoration ended the reign of Emperor Napoleon I, Artois led the ultraroyalist political faction and in

1824 would himself take the throne as Charles X. The despotism of his rule provoked his overthrow by the revolution of 1830.

A number of influential historians, including Thomas Carlyle and Jules Michelet, have lent their authority to the canard that Marat had been nothing more than a lowly veterinarian in the comte d'Artois' stables. Because Marat had identified himself on the title pages of his scientific books as "Physician to the Comte d'Artois's Company of Bodyguards," this allegation was meant to expose him as a fraud for claiming more importance than he deserved. It is definitely disproved, however, by "a glance at the Royal Almanac," where Marat "is listed as Doctor of the Body-Guard of the Count of Artois until the appointment of his successor in 1786, although he resigned in 1783."[7]

The material that purports to expose Marat as a fraudulent medical practitioner originated in the professional jealousy of academic doctors of the University of Paris's Faculty of Medicine and the Royal Society of Medicine. Evidence of their hostility to Marat has frequently been cited to demonstrate that he was not part of the recognized medical profession and had actually been shunned by it. This entry in Parisian police records reveals that his rivals even tried to have him outlawed:

MARAT: Bold charlatan. M. Vicq d'Azyr asks, in the name of the Royal Society of Medicine, that he be run out of Paris. He is from Neuchâtel in Switzerland. Many sick persons have died in his hands, but he has a doctor's degree, which was bought for him.[8]

Marat's medical enemies also tried to discredit him by submitting his "eau-factice-pulmonique"—the medicine he used to cure the marquise de l'Aubespine, and which he was selling to the general public—to chemical analysis. A report issued by Henri Alexandre Tessier, doctor-regent of the Faculty of Medicine, stated that Marat's concoction was simply chalk dissolved in water.[9] Once again, however, the charge must be considered in its proper historical context. Techniques of chemical analysis were in their infancy. The therapeutic efficacy of spa waters was routinely evaluated on purely empirical grounds. Marat's pharmacology fell within that tradition. There is no evidence of fraud on his part.

As for Marat's alleged alienation from the medical profession, it is worth considering what those who were hostile to him represented. One medical historian has described the abbé Tessier's institution, the Parisian Faculty of Medicine, as "the most formidable opponent of change and medical advance" in prerevolutionary France.[10] The medical establishment was itself divided: The Royal Society of Medicine (founded in 1776, the year Marat returned to France) and the Faculty of Medicine were at war with each other over the right to control licensing procedures that would determine who would legally be entitled to practice medicine and who would not.[11] In the years before the Revolution that was ultimately a matter of royal prerogative. Therefore, both the Faculty and the Royal Society looked to the court to sanction their authority. Marat's employment by the comte d'Artois demonstrates that he already enjoyed the court's official approval and needed neither the Faculty nor the Royal Society to ratify it. It is clear, then, that in the context of old-regime society Marat was not only a legitimate member of the medical profession, but a relatively high-ranking one.

Leaving aside his reputation and professional status, can anything be known about Marat's actual performance as a doctor or the effectiveness of his treatments? Historian of medicine Jean François Lemaire has concluded that Marat was on the leading edge of—and perhaps even in advance of—the medical revolution described by Michel Foucault in his *Birth of the Clinic*. Foucault contended that the practice of medicine made a giant leap forward when doctors stopped asking the eighteenth-century question "What's wrong with you?" and began in the early nineteenth century to ask "Where does it hurt?" instead. In the earlier tradition, physicians did not treat a patient in person; their diagnosis and prescriptions were based on a written report of the patient's complaints. The change came when doctors began to examine sick people face-to-face. According to Lemaire, Marat "broke through that frontier" not in the nineteenth century but in the 1770s at the latest. Marat, he says, was a "conscientious and knowledgeable practitioner, a pioneer clinician, and an imaginative and prudent therapist."[12]

In summary, Marat's medical credentials were genuine, his writings demonstrated medical knowledge, his treatments were state-of-the-art, he served a socially prominent clientele, and the testimony of his patients confirms that his ability to cure was at least acceptable according to contemporary norms. It is not necessary to prove that his therapies were effective or that he made lasting contributions to medical science to conclude that he was justified in presenting himself as a professional doctor in the 1770s. Accusations that he was a quack and a charlatan arose from rivalries within the nascent profession, and were magnified after the Revolution as a weapon in the ideological struggle against the revolutionary phantom that Marat had come to represent.

## THE TURN TO EXPERIMENTAL PHYSICS

In the late 1770s Marat embarked upon a major career change. He officially remained in the medical service of the comte d'Artois until 1783, but a few years earlier he had turned his attention to experimental physics, which eventually became his sole preoccupation. Throughout the 1780s, up to the eve of the Revolution, Marat dedicated himself to investigating and writing about the physical properties of heat, light, and electricity. The numerous volumes he published on these subjects report on thousands of experiments he conducted, and also attempt to offer a broad theoretical account of the phenomena he observed.

Some of his former patients admired his scientific work and helped him advance his new career as a physicist. The marquis and marquise de l'Aubespine were among Marat's most important patrons; it was at the de l'Aubespine residence in Paris that he established his laboratory. The chevalier de Joubert, treasurer-general of the estates of Languedoc, also provided laboratory space for Marat in his home in Paris. Other prominent figures who voiced support for Marat's research included the duc de

Villeroy (governor of Lyon); the comte de Tressan (lieutenant-general of the King's armies), the comte de Nogent, the comte de Wallis, the baron de Feldenfeld, and the celebrated Beaumarchais, author of *The Barber of Seville* and *The Marriage of Figaro*.

Marat's reputation as a scientist parallels that of his medical career. Despite his success in attracting wealthy and socially connected patrons to support his research, some of the leading lights of the Parisian Academy of Sciences—most notably Condorcet, Lavoisier, and Laplace—considered him a charlatan. Nonetheless, Marat enjoyed considerable prestige as a man of science among broad segments of the educated population.

After Marat's death and the downturn of the Revolution—in the period known as the Thermidorian reaction—a *légende noire* was created that sought to denigrate every aspect of his life, including his scientific career. The development of science during the French Revolution began to be interpreted in retrospect as a struggle won by partisans of modern science, symbolized by Antoine Lavoisier, over the retrograde forces of "Jacobin science," epitomized by Marat.[13]

This schema held that Marat and the other radical revolutionary leaders were implacably hostile to science. They were said to be animated by Rousseau's contention that the growth of scientific knowledge had not brought about an improvement in the human condition but had caused society to become less virtuous and less happy. Then, the story goes, during the Revolution the radicals in power put their anti-science ideology into practice by destroying the Academy of Sciences, driving its leader, Condorcet, to his death, executing the most important French scientist of the age, Lavoisier, and declaring that the Republic had no need of scientists.

The most lurid charge against Jacobin science was that Marat's blind hatred of the Academy of Sciences was responsible for Lavoisier's execution. The notion that he had a direct hand in Lavoisier's death is plainly nonsense: Lavoisier was guillotined on May 8, 1794, ten months after Marat himself had been assassinated. It has been argued, however, that Marat's earlier journalistic attacks against Lavoisier sealed his fate, but that charge also fails to stand up to scrutiny. Marat's polemics did not single Lavoisier out for special attention, and they did not focus on his role as a scientist. Lavoisier was condemned to death as one of a group of 28 wealthy financiers ("tax farmers") who had funded the operations of the royal regime. Marat's posthumous voice was but one of many in the wave of indignation that engulfed Lavoisier and his fellow tax farmers.

Nor can the political tide that swept the Academy of Sciences away be attributed to Marat's influence alone. The call for abolishing it was broad and strong. Closing the Academy was but a particular manifestation of the Revolution's general elimination of privileged corporate bodies.

## WAS MARAT A "REAL" SCIENTIST?

There is a great deal of evidence to establish that Marat was a recognized participant in the science of his day. His contributions never became a central focus of scientific discourse in France, but his work was widely known and discussed in important intellectual circles.

The most intense phase of Marat's experimental activity—from about 1778 through 1782—is extraordinarily well documented. His published works on the physics of heat, of light, and of electricity provide meticulously detailed accounts of how he performed his thousands of experiments, as well as precise illustrations of the apparatus he designed and used, and even the names of the craftsmen who constructed it for him.[14]

He conducted public demonstrations of his experiments, and attracted a loyal following. Other savants also offered public lecture series and university physics courses based on his discoveries. Among his disciples were two young men who ironically would later number among his most important political enemies, Jacques Pierre Brissot and Charles Barbaroux. Marat's books on physics, published in German as well as French,[15] were favorably reviewed by the leading journals[16] and were cited in the works of other scientists, including Academy of Sciences

members Lamarck, Lacépède, and Sage.[17] Goethe, who wrote
a multi-volume work on the physics of color perception, also
commented favorably on Marat's writings on the subject.[18]

Essay competitions sponsored by provincial academies were
an important arena of scientific discourse in late-eighteenth-
century France. Marat participated in a number of them, and
some of his submissions won prizes and honorable mention.[19]
Between 1778 and 1787 he entered contests held by the
academies of Bordeaux, Dijon, Lyon, Montpellier, and Rouen.
In 1783 his essay on the medical uses of electricity took first
prize, a gold medal valued at 300 livres, in an Academy of
Rouen competition.[20] He submitted two essays on Newtonian
color theory to a Lyon Academy competition in 1784, and
although they did not win, they were cited by the judges as the
best of those that had opposed the Newtonian view. In 1786 he
again won Rouen's first prize for an essay challenging Newton's
explanation of colors in soap bubbles.[21]

In 1783 Marat became a candidate for the presidency of a
national Academy of Sciences that was to be created in Spain.
One of Marat's wealthy patrons, Philippe Roume de Saint
Laurent, negotiated with the Spanish government on his behalf.
Spain's prime minister, Floridablanca, subsequently directed his
ambassador to France, the comte d'Aranda, to meet and interview
Marat. Meanwhile, Marat's detractors in the Parisian Academy
of Sciences were campaigning against his candidacy, and their
influence prevailed. Although he was ultimately not offered the
position, it is undeniable that he had been seriously considered.[22]

All of this would suggest that Marat was indeed a legitimate
practitioner of science as it was understood in the late eighteenth
century. But no fact that appears to put him in a positive light
has gone unchallenged by the authors and perpetuators of the
*légende noire*. It has been suggested, for example, that the
positive journal reviews of his work were written by Marat
himself, and that the recognition he received from the academies
of Rouen and Lyon was less than spontaneous. He was alleged
to have manipulated their awards committees.[23]

Marat was certainly an aggressive self-promoter; his dependence on patronage required it. It is not unlikely that he was the anonymous author of some of the glowing reviews of his own books. These journal items, however, were not supposed to be appraisals by independent reviewers, but abstracts for which the author of the abstracted work bore responsibility. Even so, praise of Marat's work could not have appeared in the journals against the will of their respective editors.

With regard to Marat's successes in the essay competitions, it has been charged that he was in cahoots with some of the provincial academies' leaders, who conspired with him in the formulation of their prize-essay topics, giving him an opening to smuggle his pet theories into the contests. What the evidence seems to show, however, is not conspiratorially rigged contests, but run-of-the-mill factionalism wherein Marat's allies sought to promote their man's ideas. This sort of cronyism, which is also evident in Marat's efforts to win the Spanish Academy of Sciences job, certainly conflicts with the noble ideal of disinterested science. At issue, however, is whether it was typical or atypical of the internal workings of provincial academies in eighteenth-century France. Considered in that light, it becomes evident that the factionalism surrounding Marat's contest entries simply represented academic politics as usual.[24]

The very fact that Marat had cronies, collaborators, or partisans in the provincial academies indicates that he was part of an intellectual milieu rather than an isolated crank. It is particularly significant that his friends in the provinces were not marginal characters, but included such highly placed figures as the duc de Villeroy and the chevalier de Joubert.

## MARAT AND THE ACADEMY OF SCIENCES

Marat's rancorous opposition to the Parisian *Académie des Sciences* during the Revolution was significant because to challenge the Academy was to challenge an important institution of the monarchy. It stood for mainstream science not only in the ideological sense, but also as the representative of the state's power of control over science. Even if Marat had never engaged in scientific pursuits himself, it would surely have been among his political targets. But his personal experience with the institution gave specific form to his attack, which was expressed most fully in a long pamphlet he published in September 1791 entitled *Les Charlatans Modernes*.[25]

Because Marat's relationship with the Academy ended in bitter mutual recriminations, most historians have assumed that his scientific work was poorly received in general. That conclusion is flawed in three regards. First, it overlooks the earlier positive reception accorded him by the Academy. Second, it treats the Academy as if it were the entire scientific community rather than simply the elite of that community. And third, it exaggerates the monolithism of the Academy in the prerevolutionary era.

At the outset of his career as a physicist, Marat's relations with the Parisian Academy were not at all antagonistic. The Academy twice appointed official commissions to evaluate his work. In the first episode, a famous international associate member of the Academy, Benjamin Franklin, joined academicians Le Roy and Sage in a series of visits to witness demonstrations of Marat's solar microscope.[26] The official report of this first commission was highly favorable to Marat.[27] The second time around, however, did not go as smoothly. This time academicians Le Roy and Cousin examined a lengthy series of Marat's optical experiments and their subsequent report was pointedly brief and noncommittal.[28] By the middle of 1780 Marat's relationship with the Academy had soured and by 1782 it was ruined beyond repair.

One of the main elements in Marat's alienation from the Academy was his overt opposition to Newton's optical theories. Newton's prestige was so high that his works were treated as inviolable dogma, which caused Marat's critique to be dismissed out of hand as scientific heresy. The elite among the academicians denounced Marat for his audacity, and almost all historians of science have echoed that judgment ever since.

One significant exception is Charles C. Gillispie, who despite an acknowledged aversion to Marat was able to fair-mindedly evaluate his critique of Newtonian optics. Examining the subject in historical perspective, Gillispie concluded that some of Marat's criticisms were "far from empty," and that the Academy's report failed to give them the attention they merited.[29] With regard to Marat's claim that Newton idealized his accounts of his experimental procedures, Gillispie says that Marat's suspicions "come closer to an accurate intuition about the kind of window-dressing Newton sometimes put around his findings than does anything known to me in the eighteenth-century literature."[30]

Furthermore, while almost all previous historians who had written on the subject had assumed that when Marat translated Newton's *Opticks* into French in 1786 he must have somehow dishonestly imported his own contrarian views into it, Gillispie dissented, saying it is "an excellent translation." A careful comparison to Newton's text, he added, "requires it to be said in all fairness that he was nowhere unfaithful to Newton's meaning."[31] The excellence of Marat's translation is underscored by the remarkable fact that it was in print more than two centuries later.[32]

The antagonistic relationship that developed between Marat and the Academy of Sciences was not a case of irrational professional jealousy on his part, as many commentators have argued, but was a result of mutual incompatibility. On the one hand Lavoisier, Condorcet, and Laplace, among others, were fully convinced that Marat was simply a charlatan. Marat was no less convinced that Lavoisier, Condorcet, and Laplace were charlatans, using their institutional authority as a shield against the scrutiny of their science by independent scientists such as himself. There was no common ground on which their differences could have been resolved. The Academy attempted to banish Marat from the scientific community, but the Revolution instead drove the Academy out of existence.

Evaluating the charges of charlatanism that Marat and Lavoisier hurled against each other, historians have frequently reasoned that because Lavoisier is an acknowledged giant of

modern science, Marat was obviously in the wrong, and therefore
Lavoisier's characterization of Marat must have been correct.
The two propositions are not logically connected, however;
neither was justified in calling the other a charlatan.


## THE WINDING DOWN OF MARAT'S SCIENTIFIC CAREER

Marat had apparently been able to make a good enough living as
an experimental physicist to allow him to hobnob with the rich
and famous, at least through the middle of the 1780s. It seems
peculiar, given his later political trajectory, that he would have
had a personal servant, but he did indeed for a time employ a
young man named Nicolas Dumoulin as a lackey.[33]

It is possible, but not certain, that in the later years of the
decade preceding the Revolution he saw a downturn in his
fortunes. The hostility of the Academy of Sciences may have
damaged his ability to function as a physicist by making it
more difficult for him to attract patronage. Some historians
have hypothesized that Marat's "failure" as a scientist was the
motivation for his revolutionary fervor. It drove him to madness
and despair, they suggest, and to crave revenge against the
society that had failed to appreciate his genius.[34] This conjecture,
however, is based on thin evidence. An examination of Marat's
journalistic output from 1789 to the end of his life refutes the
charge that he continued to be obsessed with hatred and jealousy
of the Academy of Sciences, and with Lavoisier in particular.
His writings on that subject account for but a tiny portion of
his total body of work.

That Marat's personal antipathy toward the Academy of
Sciences did not influence his political judgment is demonstrated
by his attitude toward Antoine Fourcroy, who was Lavoisier's
closest ally in the field of chemistry. Marat lambasted Fourcroy
for his role in the Academy, but nonetheless publicly supported
his candidacy for election to the Convention.[35] Ironically,
Fourcroy would later occupy the seat in the Convention vacated
by Marat's assassination.

It is likely that Marat suffered from a serious illness in 1788. He later said he believed he had been on his deathbed at that time.[36] If so, it may well have caused a deterioration in his financial situation, but none of this is known with certainty. In any event, the contention that Marat's revolutionary spirit was the product of a disturbed mind had its unfounded origins in the *légende noire*.

# 3

# From the Estates General
# to the King's Flight
## January 1789 to June 1791

At the beginning of 1789 Marat's scientific career had reached an apparent dead end. The serious illness that had afflicted him the previous summer seems to have sapped him of the energy necessary to combat the hostility of the Academy of Sciences leaders. Fearing he was near death, he wrote his will and named a friend, Abraham Louis Bréguet, as the executor.[1]

His illness was certainly not entirely psychosomatic—he had long suffered from a painful skin disease then generally considered incurable and fatal[2]—but it may well have been exacerbated by psychological depression. If so, the first stirrings of the coming Revolution shook him out of it. "I was on my deathbed," he later wrote, "when a friend ... told me about the convocation of the Estates General. This news had a powerful effect on me; my illness suddenly broke and my spirits revived."[3]

## HOW THE REVOLUTION BEGAN

Because Marat's activities during the final four years of his life were so intimately intertwined with the events of the French Revolution, an appreciation of its ebbs, flows, and crashing waves is essential to understanding how Marat became its emblematic figure. The Revolution was a series of popular explosions that ultimately destroyed the traditional social structure of France and cleared the way for the transformation of Europe and the world.

The beginning of any chain of historical causation is impossible to pinpoint, but a good argument can be made that the French Revolution began with the American Revolution. The government of France had gone deeply into debt supporting the Americans' struggle against England. Its finances were stretched to the breaking point; approximately half of its budget was going for interest on its loans.

The King's ministers launched a frantic search for new sources of revenue. Raising the taxes of the peasants, who accounted for at least 95 percent of the population, could only produce minimal returns because they were already so heavily taxed that little more could be squeezed out of them. The monarchy was thus compelled to increase the level of taxation of the aristocratic class, which had traditionally enjoyed extensive exemption from taxes.

Not surprisingly, the nobles resisted this challenge to the economic status quo. Despite their privileged position in *ancien régime* society, the aristocrats had long been excluded from a direct political role in governing France. To defend themselves against the threat of higher taxes, they began to campaign for more political rights. Their challenge to the monarchy, however, was more successful than they had bargained for. This "aristocratic rebellion" inadvertently opened the door for other social classes to also raise demands. The great irony of the French Revolution is that the social class that touched it off was the one ultimately destroyed by it.

The process of the Revolution has been described as a succession of four overlapping revolutionary waves crashing against the monarchy. In the wake of the aristocratic rebellion, the bourgeoisie (the incipient capitalist class) joined the fray, and then the peasants, and finally the urban poor for whom Marat became the tribune.[4] The French Revolution was thus not simply a struggle between two clearly counterposed groups, with oppressed people on one side and their oppressors on the other. Those who set out to challenge the monarchy included a broad range of social forces from the very wealthy to the desperately poor. The unity of this coalition did not survive the Revolution's earliest successes, which satisfied some of the rebels but left others deeply dissatisfied. The former then sought to stabilize and defend the new status quo against those who, like Marat, fought to extend the Revolution.

## THE ESTATES GENERAL AND THE THIRD ESTATE

The aristocrats' campaign for political representation led them to demand the reconvening of the Estates General, a medieval predecessor of modern parliaments that had last been seen in France in 1614, a century and a half earlier. The Estates General was not a democratic institution; it was composed of three "estates" with vastly unequal voting power. The three estates had one vote each despite the fact that the First Estate (the clergy) represented some 100,000 people, the Second Estate (the nobility) about 400,000, and the Third Estate (everybody else) about 25 million. Because the clergy was completely under the control of the aristocracy, on all significant issues the nobles would outvote the commoners two-to-one every time.

Nevertheless, the aristocrats' demand for an Estates General was taken up by all sections of the population because it was a serious challenge to an unpopular monarchy. In late 1788 the royal government, weakened by the fiscal crisis, acceded to the pressure and on May 5, 1789, the Estates General was convened. The representatives of the Third Estate, however, had been energized by the agitation and were not inclined to accept the traditional one-vote-per-estate structure. They demanded that the voting instead reflect the real numerical strength of their constituency. When the nobles refused, the Third Estate's leaders held their own meeting, and on June 17 declared themselves the National Assembly.

The significance of this event cannot be overstated. The National Assembly represented the advent of *dual power* in France—the rise of a new organ of governmental power in competition with the monarchy. Although it consisted almost entirely of men from the urban "middle classes" (professional people, intellectuals, small proprietors, and so forth), it was supported by the overwhelming majority of the population.

In late 1788 when the royal government issued the call for the Estates General, it had also invited people of all social classes and walks of life to express their opinions on how to improve the social order. The King's ministers apparently felt that doing so would be a harmless way to give the people the impression they were being listened to. If so, they miscalculated, because the response was far greater than anticipated. Sixty thousand lists of grievances (*cahiers de doléances*) flooded in from every part of the realm.

## MARAT AWAKENS

Meanwhile, the great social ferment had rekindled Marat's enthusiasm for life and restored him to health. He responded to the call for the *cahiers* by writing and publishing an anonymous pamphlet entitled *Offering to the Nation*.[5] It came off the presses in late January 1789, marking Marat's final career change— from physicist to revolutionary journalist and politician. Over the next few months this minor member of the intelligentsia would become a figure celebrated and reviled throughout France and beyond as the fearsome People's Friend, scourge and worst nightmare of all privileged classes.

How did this happen? In early 1789 Marat was a political unknown. He was elected to neither the Estates General nor the new municipal governing body, the Paris Commune, and his was but one in a cacophony of agitational voices striving to attract a mass following. What was it about Marat that enabled him to stand out from the others and advance to the forefront of public attention by year's end?

His first contribution to the political ferment, the 62-page *Offering to the Nation*, was not especially radical, either in content or tone, and attracted little notice. Reformist rather than revolutionary, it simply proposed a series of reforms aimed at bringing about peaceful social change. In it, Marat explicitly rejected revolutionary aims. "Blessed be the best of Kings!" he exclaimed; it is only "the enemies of the nation" who "howl for innovations and for the overthrow of the monarchy."[6] However, he added, sovereignty must ultimately belong to the elected representatives of the nation, "which alone must make the fundamental laws of the State."[7] He blamed former royal officials, especially Calonne, for leading France into a terrible mess, but at the same time praised the current finance minister, Jacques Necker, as a "great statesman" whose "integrity inspires confidence."[8]

Although *Offering to the Nation* was generally moderate, it did contain hints of the ideas that would soon distinguish Marat from other polemicists. A footnote warned would-be oppressors and the wealthy "who peacefully enjoy all the advantages of society" to think twice before "pushing to the point of despair an immense and courageous people who at present are demanding no more than a little solace for their pains; who still ask for nothing more than a legal system committed to justice."[9]

Later in January the King issued an official call to convoke the electors to choose representatives to the Estates General. In early March Marat responded to the Royal Letters with another anonymous pamphlet, *Supplement to the Offering to the Nation*, which continued in the same reformist vein.[10] "Father of the People!" he exclaimed rhetorically to the monarch; "Help us break our chains! Lead us to our freedom!" This time, however, Marat seemed considerably less optimistic. He expressed disappointment with the King's message. Rather than focusing on the social crisis plaguing the nation, all it contained was the "all-too-ordinary language of an imperious prince" concerned only with the crisis of the royal finances.[11]

The *Supplement* drew directly from Marat's political writings of 15 years earlier in England. It contained long passages from his *Chains of Slavery* and restated many of the same themes. "The interests of the privileged orders," Marat wrote, "are incompatible with the interests of the people; it is upon the degradation, oppression, humiliation, and misery of the vast majority that a small minority bases its elevation, domination, glory, and happiness." Most contemptible, in Marat's eyes, were the self-styled "reasonable men" who passively observe the "suffering of the oppressed and the agony of the poor crushed by hunger" and who "open their mouths only to counsel patience and moderation."[12] In spite of its darker tone, however, Marat's second pamphlet ended with the hope that Louis XVI's "beautiful soul" would "make justice reign and render his people happy."[13]

It may seem inconsistent of Marat to simultaneously criticize and laud the King, but it was entirely conventional in the pre-Revolutionary political context. Marat, along with almost everyone else in France, was a monarchist because he believed that the only alternative to centralized executive power was anarchy, and he was no anarchist. Having one individual who could act as the ultimate decision maker was assumed to be a social necessity, and the only person who could possibly wield the necessary authority was Louis XVI. But in Marat's eyes the King's power would only be legitimate if constrained by law and exercised in the interests of the people.

Although Marat's *Supplement* was far from a call to rebellion, its message was critical enough to catch the eye of the royal censors. It was declared seditious, and on March 12 a police order was issued to seize all copies. This was the first action taken against Marat by the police, and it backfired. Instead of silencing him, it brought him to the attention of the radicalizing public. It established his credentials as a militant patriot and helped him win election to his district's electoral committee. Thus began a recurring theme wherein police repression would give Marat the aura of an unjustly persecuted patriot and burnish his reputation as a courageous partisan of the Revolution.

Marat's first political victory was his election to the committee of the Carmes-Déchaussés district, where he lived. For the elections to the Estates General, Paris had been divided into 60 districts. Public assemblies open to all residents were held in each district for the purpose of electing a committee that would choose the Parisian representatives of the Third Estate. The district assembly meetings, however, soon took on a political life of their own, and the district committees developed into activist organizations that began to exercise political power on the local level.

Exactly what Marat did as a member of the Carmes-Déchaussés district committee is not known. Aside from the agitational effects of his pamphlets, he never claimed an organizational or leadership role in the period leading up to the first great outburst of the Revolution—the insurrection at the Bastille on July 14.

## THE ORIGINAL BASTILLE DAY

In that summer of 1789 a new political atmosphere of hope and raised expectations pervaded Paris after the representatives of the Third Estate had declared themselves the National Assembly. At the same time, a sense of foreboding was in the air due to persistent rumors of aristocratic plots against the newborn Revolution. The resulting fears and insecurity, combined with a steep rise in the price of bread that threatened widespread starvation, brought the masses of Parisian artisans and tradespeople to the point of open rebellion.

The spark that touched off the revolt was the royal government's dismissal of the finance minister, Necker, whom Marat had praised in his first pamphlet. Necker had been widely perceived as a champion of economic reform, so the dashed hopes represented by his dismissal on July 11 prompted the outbreak of insurrection on July 12. The outburst was not entirely spontaneous; the district organizations played a role in preparing and mobilizing the Parisian population. Angry crowds armed themselves by looting gunsmiths' shops. Political leaders of the Third Estate sought to bring order to the revolt by organizing a citizens' militia, the National Guard. Because the ranks of the royal army had been affected by the widespread revolutionary sentiment, their commanders prudently confined the troops to their barracks.

The tumultuous action in the streets of Paris reached its climax on July 14 with the celebrated assault on the Bastille. The old prison was being used as an armory, and the crowd proceeded to confiscate its guns and ammunition. The uprising quickly triumphed. The existing municipal administration was pushed aside and replaced by a new city government, the Paris Commune. The National Guard was officially established and placed under the command of a popular military hero, the marquis de Lafayette. Necker was reinstated as finance minister, and Louis XVI was obliged to symbolically acknowledge the Revolution's victory by donning the tricolor cockade, to the cheers of the Parisian masses.

The insurrection had validated the rule of the National Assembly and inaugurated a period of *de facto* constitutional monarchy. Paris's new city government was based on a democratically elected council. The elections took place at the district level; the 60 districts each sent five delegates to make up the 300-member assembly. Marat was not among them. As news of the great Parisian insurrection spread, similar uprisings took place in cities all across the country and established the rule of revolutionary committees.

Meanwhile, in rural France, the peasants saw the weakening of the royal regime as an opportunity to redress their own grievances. Oppressed for centuries by feudal dues, taxes, tithes, and forced labor, they rose up throughout the countryside against their aristocratic *seigneurs*. The sacking and burning of manor houses was the most dramatic image of the rural revolt, but far more important was that they had occurred at harvest time and forcibly prevented the collection of dues, taxes, and tithes. A primary target of the peasants' fires was their landlords' archives, where the documents defining their obligations had been kept.

## MARAT'S PARTICIPATION IN THE FIRST INSURRECTION

Marat later wrote about what he had been doing on the fateful day of July 14. He did not claim to have been among the crowd that stormed the Bastille, but says that during the ensuing turmoil he happened upon a large contingent of German soldiers on the Pont Neuf, one of the bridges over the Seine in the center of Paris. Their commanding officer was addressing a crowd, saying that he and his troops were there to fight alongside the Parisian people. His listeners applauded, but Marat smelled a rat. "I jumped up and dashed through the crowd," he says. "I denounced these troops as traitors who had come to massacre us in our sleep."[14]

According to his account, Marat succeeded in winning over the crowd, which forced the German troops to surrender their arms. He claimed he had thus "aborted the treasonous project of surprising Paris with several detachments of German infantry and cavalry."[15] The implication is that had he not acted, the newborn Revolution might well have been crushed in its cradle.

There is no independent evidence that corroborates Marat's story, and some historians have dismissed it as pure falsehood. Nonetheless, Marat cited eyewitnesses by name and none ever came forward to contradict it, although some most likely would have done so had he simply made it up. It seems reasonable to conclude that some such incident did occur, but perhaps was not the crucially important event Marat believed it to have been.

Following the confrontation with the German troops, Marat says, he returned to the Carmes-Déchaussés district headquarters. The district committee was in permanent session and he worked around the clock, continuously, for three days and nights. The task at hand for all of the districts was to organize the National Guard as a permanent militia capable of militarily defending their Revolution. On the evening of Friday, July 17, Marat headed home at last to sleep.

On the morning of Sunday, July 19, he returned to the headquarters to present a proposal to the committee. Marat had decided that the most valuable contribution he could make to the Revolution was with his pen, so he proposed that the district publish a political journal and offered his own services as its editor. His motion was voted down, however, because the committee's majority felt that there were already enough revolutionary publications in circulation. Although Marat took this rebuff calmly, he later said that it prompted him to resign from the district committee in order to found a political journal on his own.

Had the district agreed to sponsor a publication, it would have provided the presses, paper, ink, typesetters, printers, and distributors, but without its backing Marat had to shoulder the entire burden of production by himself. He managed to do so by "living economically in humble circumstances," he says. "For the past nine months I have subsisted on bread and water in order to bear the expenses of printing, which have become exorbitant."[16]

On August 11, a month after striking off on his own, his new publication, the *Moniteur Patriote*, made its debut, but it was short-lived. The following month, however, he started it up again under a different name, and this time was able to keep it going. On September 12 the first issue of the journal that would from then on be associated with Marat's name came off the presses: the *Ami du peuple*—the *People's Friend*. It was a daily newspaper with initial press runs of about 2,000 copies. Marat's production costs have been estimated at about 80 to 90 livres per issue, the approximate equivalent of a month's wages for an unskilled worker, or the price of a meal for four at a fashionable Parisian restaurant.[17] At the beginning, *Ami du peuple* seems to have survived by means of credit at high interest rates from printers and distributors, but after it became popular it certainly could have generated enough income to cover the cost of its production.[18]

The influence of Marat's journal cannot be measured by the size of its press run, because its audience was many times larger. Individual copies of the paper were passed from hand to hand and read aloud in public squares and coffeehouses. One contemporary commentator estimated that each single copy of popular periodicals was read by ten people.[19] Nonetheless, the press runs of Marat's journal increased along with its growing influence, reaching a maximum of perhaps 6,000. The size of the press runs was not determined by economic demand, but by the physical limitations of eighteenth-century printing technology. To produce three to six thousand copies of a newspaper on a daily basis, one historian estimates, "was a task calculated to keep three to five simple hand presses busy for virtually the entire working week."[20] At times *Ami du peuple* came off the presses simultaneously at three different printshops in order to reach the 6,000-copies-a-day level.[21]

Meanwhile, the great political transformation was unfolding all around him, so Marat had much more on his mind than the mere technical aspects of launching a periodical. Between July and September he was engaged in observing and analyzing the political scene and trying to find ways to make his opinions heard. A first major task confronting the new order was to legitimize itself by codifying its principles. The National Assembly appointed a committee to write a draft constitution, and Marat followed its deliberations with intense interest. In addition to presenting his ideas to the public in pamphlet form, by his own count he submitted more than 20 documents directly to the National Assembly delegates, but never received a response.

## THE NIGHT OF AUGUST 4

Less than a month after Bastille Day, on Tuesday, August 4, a very strange session of the National Assembly took place. Noblemen paraded to the podium, one after another, to voluntarily renounce their aristocratic privileges, and the National Assembly officially decreed the end of feudalism. Most contemporary commentators took the declarations at face value, but Marat did not. In a pamphlet entitled *A Project to Deceive the People*, he concluded that the concessions were illusory. "Don't let anybody fool you," he wrote. If the aristocratic landowners

> made these sacrifices out of the goodness of their hearts, why did it take them so long to raise their voices? Their mansions were in flames and they had the great generosity to renounce the privilege of holding in chains people who had already gained their freedom, arms in hand![22]

In other words, the nobles were only surrendering rights and privileges that had already come under sharp attack by the peasants' revolt. They were trying to put the best spin possible on events that had escaped their control.

The destruction of the legal framework of feudal society was of immense historical significance, but Marat was accurate in his contention that the nobles had no intention of making fundamental material sacrifices. They were seeking to convert their no longer viable feudal privileges into a more effective form of property: money. The peasants would have to pay for their emancipation, and the National Assembly supported the nobles' demand for compensation. Feudal dues would be legally eliminated, but only in exchange for cash payments. Because few peasants had the wherewithal to pay the amounts in question, they were faced with being in debt to their former landlords and paying off the "loans" in perpetuity.

The peasants, of course, were certainly not satisfied with this result. They continued their struggle, often in open rebellion to the point of civil war, for four more years, until in 1793 they won a more fundamental victory. It was then that a more radical legislative body, the Jacobin-dominated Convention, declared the peasants' redemptive debts null and void.

Marat finished writing his commentary on the August 4 session two days after it occurred, but it only appeared in print in September, after he had established his own journal and was able to publish it himself. Before that, he had found that printers were hesitant to take him on as a client; he complained bitterly of their "pusillanimity." This was an indication that Marat's political agitation was beginning to run ahead of events. Whereas most partisans of the Revolution were euphoric over the aristocrats' "surrender," he was denouncing it as nothing but a trick.

He had more luck finding a printer for another pamphlet—*The Constitution, or Proposal for a Declaration of the Rights of Man and of the Citizen*—which was published on August 23.[23] He submitted this detailed analysis of what a new constitution should contain to the National Assembly, which paid it no attention, just as it had ignored all of his previous suggestions. This pamphlet again exhibited the combination of political moderation and social radicalism that had distinguished Marat's first writings of 1789. He continued to believe that "monarchical government is the only form of government suitable for France," while at the same time putting forward a definition of human and civil rights that far surpassed mere equality before the law. Political freedom, he insisted, is meaningless to a starving person; genuine freedom requires the abolition of poverty.

Marat did not challenge the right to private property, but he maintained that people without property who were faced with starving to death had an *absolute natural right* to confiscate the surplus property of the wealthy.[24] There were two ways, he said, that the constitution could codify that. Preferably, "the law should forbid excessive inequality of wealth; limitations should be imposed and strictly enforced." But if limiting the accumulation of wealth were to be rejected, then at the very least, "society owes guaranteed subsistence to its propertyless members."[25]

Most of the members of the constitutional committee undoubtedly perceived Marat's quasi-communistic notions—if they were even aware of them—as absurd and out of touch with reality. On August 26, 1789, the National Assembly as a whole issued its historic Declaration of the Rights of Man and the Citizen. Basic democratic rights—freedom of speech, freedom of the press, freedom from arbitrary arrest, and religious freedom—became the law of the land. But at the same time, the Declaration also affirmed the inviolability and sacredness of *property* rights, underlining the social character—and limitations—of the Revolution at that stage of its development. Its aim was to promote personal liberty and civil equality, not social equality.

Everyone who supported the Revolution favored the struggle for *égalité*, but the word did not mean the same thing to everyone. To relatively well-off people it meant eliminating the legal and economic privileges of the hereditary nobility. Above all, it signified equal rights with regard to owning property and accumulating wealth. For people of more humble economic status, however, equality *included* equal rights before the law, but it also entailed eliminating the distinction between the wealthy and the poor. The tension between these incompatible ideals has been a feature of all modern revolutions, from seventeenth-century England to twentieth-century China, and the French Revolution was no exception. Marat's unique place in history stems from his having been the French Revolution's most consistent and resolute champion of social equality.

## MARAT'S FIRST RUN-IN WITH THE NEW AUTHORITIES

By August the Parisian police were under the *de facto* control of the new municipal government, the Paris Commune. Officially, however, they remained under the jurisdiction of the Châtelet, a judicial institution of the monarchy. To the public, then, both the royal government and the new city government bore responsibility for the actions of the police. In mid-August, when Marat found himself once again under attack from the police, his counterattack simultaneously condemned the repression of the old regime and the collaborationism of the new regime.

This time, ironically, his run-in with the police began with an attempt on his part to avoid legal problems. His earlier experience with timid printers led him to conclude that they needed some form of official assurance before printing something they thought might get them in trouble. With that in mind, on August 12 Marat went to the *Hôtel de ville*, City Hall, to request permission to publish a journal. A minor official told him that no permission was required because Parisians enjoyed complete freedom of the press. Marat demanded that he put it in writing, but the functionary refused, triggering a boisterous dispute that resulted in the police being called. Marat was charged with disturbing the peace and given a summons to appear before the city council to answer the charges.

The following evening both Marat and the functionary told their stories to the 300 members of the city council. The council dismissed the charges against Marat, but refused to issue him the special authorization he wanted for his journal, fearing that it could be misinterpreted as an official seal of approval of the journal's contents. Again he was assured that all restrictions on the freedom of publication were a thing of the past.[26]

This first minor skirmish with the new municipal government ended in an apparent draw, but it nonetheless represented a small victory for Marat. The most politically active layer of the population had been made aware of Jean Paul Marat and his new journal, and the seeds of his reputation as an ardent defender of the Revolution had been planted.

Marat did not trust the assurances that the existing press freedom was unlimited, and he fully intended to probe the limitations, so his insistence on prior guarantees was a way of preparing for future battles. With persistence he eventually persuaded the police to issue him a *distribution* permit, which he reproduced in his journal as proof of its legitimacy.

## THE *AMI DU PEUPLE* ENTERS THE STAGE

Marat's new journal made its debut on September 12, 1789. Its masthead read *Publiciste Parisien*, but that name lasted only four days. On September 16 it became the *Ami du peuple*, and despite interruptions and further name changes, it would remain the instrument of his revolutionary views to the last day of his life.

*Ami du peuple* was not simply the name of a newspaper. From the beginning it was also the name of a fictional character who embodied the virtues of the ideal revolutionary patriot. The People's Friend was courageous, determined, devoted to justice, and armed with an unerring political "sixth sense" that allowed him to penetrate lies and deceptions and see through to the underlying political reality.

The "people" whom Marat sought to befriend were the revolutionary class, the *sans-culottes*. The term *sans-culottes* designated men who wore the ankle-length pants of a worker instead of the knee-length *culottes* of a gentleman. They were "the workshop masters, craftsmen, wage-earners, shopkeepers, and petty traders" of Paris.[27] "The Revolution," Marat wrote, "has been made and sustained only by the lowest classes of society—the workers, the artisans, the retailers, the farmers—by the plebeians, by those unfortunates whom the rich impudently call the rabble."[28]

## Nᵒ. V I.

# L'AMI DU PEUPLE,

O U

## LE PUBLICISTE PARISIEN,

JOURNAL POLITIQUE, LIBRE ET IMPARTIAL,

PAR UNE SOCIÉTÉ DE PATRIOTES,

*ET rédigé par M. MARAT, Auteur de L'OFFRANDE
A LA PATRIE, du MONITEUR, & du PLAN
DE CONSTITUTION , &c.*

Vitam impendere vero.

## VERSAILLES.

*Du Mercredi* 16 *Septembre* 1789.

ASSEMBLÉE NATIONALE.

Séance du 14 ſoir.

*Déciſion priſe par l'Aſſemblée de prier le Roi de
ſanctionner & faire promulguer les arrêtés des* 4
*&* 5 *Août.*
*Décret portant que la perſonne du Roi eſt ſacrée.*

F

Front cover of Marat's journal. The September 16, 1789 issue
was the first to bear the name *L'Ami du peuple*.

At first Marat identified himself in the paper as "Marat, editeur de l'*Ami du peuple*." But when letters to the editor routinely addressed *him* as the People's Friend, Marat began to identify with the character. He shortened his signature to "Marat, l'Ami du peuple" and became the People's Friend, to himself no less than to his readers.

At some point early on, Marat's journalism ceased to be essentially reformist and became explicitly revolutionary. For a while, both perspectives coexisted in his writing, but soon after he launched *Ami du peuple*, he stopped calling for reforms in the existing political order and began to call for its overthrow. Although in September 1789 almost everyone considered the National Assembly and the Paris Commune to be the institutional embodiment of the Revolution, Marat loudly insisted that the two governmental bodies were *enemies* of the Revolution. He foresaw the coming of a "second revolution" because the political domination of wealth in the current system made it impossible for the poor to achieve social justice by peaceful means. The *sans-culottes* had already successfully revolted against the nobility. Why would they not also rise up in arms against the rich?

*Ami du peuple* very quickly began to differentiate itself from competing revolutionary journals. The spectrum of opinion among them ranged from those believing that the July 14 insurrection had completed the Revolution and those believing that the Revolution had only taken a first step. *Ami du peuple* was at the latter end of the spectrum, while most others fell somewhere between the two poles. Marat's periodical thus began to attract attention, both from the radicalizing public and from the new officialdom that was increasingly pilloried in its pages. Less than two weeks after the journal's inception, Marat had already succeeded in infuriating the municipal government and on September 25 was once again subpoenaed to appear before the city council.

The most pressing political issue of the moment was the price of bread. Bread was the staple of the *sans-culottes*' diet and a sharp rise in its price threatened large numbers of people with increasing hunger and possible starvation. Food riots and violent demonstrations erupted in Paris's poorer districts. The Paris Commune organized a Subsistence Committee to address the crisis. Marat had scandalized the city government by portraying its Subsistence Committee not as part of the solution but as a major part of the problem. He accused it of conspiring with the flour-millers' guild and the royal finance minister, Jacques Necker, to hoard grain, thus forcing the price of bread sky-high. He condemned the millers as greedy profiteers, and accused Necker, whom he had warmly applauded only a few months earlier, of masterminding the conspiracy in order to discredit the Revolution and ultimately destroy it.

On September 25, Marat was ordered to appear at a hearing at City Hall,[29] at which the city council no doubt intended to demand that he cease his inflammatory rhetoric. When he arrived he was told to wait in an anteroom. Hours later, at midnight, he was informed that the council would not see him that day, but that he should come back the following day, and he did so. After passing another full day in the waiting room, however, he was told once again that he would have to return the next day.

Although Marat knew he had been summoned there to be attacked, he had planned to turn the tables on the city council by telling it how to purge itself of traitorous elements. He had reason to believe that deputies from the less-well-to-do districts would defend him and treat his accusations seriously. But after two days of sitting in the waiting room, Marat had had his fill of their maneuvers. Rather than returning again for a third day, he decided to go public. He published an open letter to the city council in the September 28 issue of *Ami du peuple*, expressing his disappointment at not having been given the opportunity to address the assembly. He said it should hear his accusations and act on them. And to emphasize his disdain for the city council he offered a comparison of their relative importance: "I am the eye of the people," he told them, "and you are at most its little finger."[30]

The city council responded immediately by ordering Marat to appear before it that evening, and this time he was received without having to wait. The president of the assembly demanded that Marat either make his accusations specific or withdraw them. Marat offered only the same generalized denunciations of the Subsistence Committee that had appeared in his articles. Following an angry exchange, what happened afterward was anticlimactic. No charges were brought against Marat—which he interpreted as a tacit admission that his accusations were accurate—and he was simply allowed to leave.[31]

This affair gave another boost to Marat's growing reputation as a spokesman for the little people against the social elite, including the *new* social elite that had been elevated by the Revolution. As time went by, his readers brought him more and more "insider information," giving him the ability to make his accusations ever more precise. Marat's rise out of obscurity had begun.

## THE OCTOBER DAYS

When Marat claimed to be "the eye of the people," he was alluding to his journal's role as an ever-vigilant sentinel keeping an eye out for counterrevolutionary plots menacing the Revolution. In the October 5, 1789 issue of *Ami du peuple* he printed a report about a "counterrevolutionary orgy" that one of his many confidential sources had witnessed at the royal court at Versailles. It was a detailed account of an incident wherein a "great number of officers" of the royal army and "leaders of the bourgeois militia" (the National Guard) had openly insulted and threatened the Revolution.[32] This was evidence supporting the persistent rumors of conspiratorial intrigue aimed at crushing the Revolution militarily.

Such reports were taken very seriously by ordinary Parisians, who lived in constant fear of being slaughtered by royalist troops. Marat exhorted his readers to rise up in arms, march on Versailles, and compel the King and his family to leave that "nest of intrigue" and permanently establish their residence in

Paris. That call appeared in *Ami du peuple* on the morning of October 5; later that same day the people responded in force.

The first insurrectionary uprising since Bastille Day convulsed Paris. Militant women were in the forefront. A huge crowd, largely made up of women armed with broomsticks, pitchforks, swords, and muskets set off on the 15-mile march from Paris to Versailles. About 20,000 men, including large numbers of National Guardsmen, brought up the rear. Lafayette was nominally their leader, but in a political sense it would be more accurate to say that he was struggling to keep up with his troops.[33] When the marchers reached Versailles the vastly outnumbered forces guarding the royal palace capitulated, leaving the King no choice but to obey the crowd's demand. He and his family were escorted to Paris by the jubilant throng and installed in the Tuileries palace.

The People's Friend claimed credit for saving the nation by "unmasking in advance the dark plot of the aristocrats" and "preparing the insurrection that took place."[34] Although other journalists, including Marat's friend Camille Desmoulins, had also promoted the October Days action, this was not an empty boast. The successful mobilization was a milestone in Marat's revolutionary career. It was the first time his agitation had made a significant impact on an event of historic importance.

In the aftermath of the October Days some of the popular journalists, including Marat's former comrade Jacques Pierre Brissot, expressed discomfort with some aspects of the mass mobilization. They reprimanded the marchers for committing acts of violence. Marat, by contrast, wholeheartedly defended them:

> The people only rise up in revolt when they are pushed to the point of despair by tyranny ... Anyway, can there be any comparison between the few victims that the people sacrifice to justice during an insurrection and the innumerable mass of subjects that a despot massacres or reduces to poverty?[35]

Social progress, he maintained, can never be accomplished without actions of the kind that occurred on October 5: "To

what do we owe our freedom if not to the popular uprisings?"
He dismissed the notion that the Revolution could be advanced
by parliamentary means as a delusion. "Study the work of the
National Assembly and you will find that it never acts except
as a response to some popular uprising."[36]

Marat berated those of his fellow journalists who had focused
their attention on peripheral cases of individual violence:

> Oh, what sensitive souls! They can see only the misfortunes of a few
> individuals who were victims of a momentary insurrection ... As for me,
> I can only see the evils, the calamities, the disaster of a great nation
> in the clutches of tyrants—chained, pilloried, tortured, oppressed, and
> massacred *for whole centuries*. Now, who is more reasonable, more
> humane—them or me? They try to lull the nation to sleep; I try to wake
> it up. They give the nation opium; I slap alcohol on its wounds.[37]

With the royal family obliged to live in Paris under the close
scrutiny of patriotic citizens, Louis XVI made a pretense of
accepting a constitutionally limited role. The threat of counterrevolution had apparently been neutralized and a period of social
peace ensued that lasted a year and a half. Throughout 1790 and
the first half of 1791, class antagonisms subsided and a general
mood of social unity prevailed. One of the few voices warning
Parisians not to drop their guard was that of the People's Friend.
Marat tirelessly hammered away on the conjoined themes that
the calm was illusory and that the Revolution was far from over.

## FORCED INTO HIDING

The municipal authorities had become increasingly wary of the
growing effectiveness of Marat's agitation. On October 3, two
days before the turbulent march on Versailles, the city council
ordered a police crackdown against him and his journal. The
events of October 5 further frightened them and stiffened their
resolve. On October 6 a printer in Marat's employ was arrested
and soon thereafter a warrant for Marat's arrest was issued.[38]

In the dark of night on October 8 the police descended upon his residence at Vieux Colombier Street, but did not find him at home. Forewarned, he had fled.

The decision to go underground was a critical juncture in Marat's revolutionary career. His journal had been published openly for less than a month—from September 12 through October 8—and already he had apparently exhausted the possibilities of the existing press freedoms. Before going into hiding he told his readers that the People's Friend had "crossed the Rubicon; he takes this step without flinching."[39]

Marat would remain in clandestinity and semiclandestinity for almost three years, until August 1792. His skill at frustrating the police in their attempts to capture him added the mystique of Robin Hood to the already mythic reputation of the People's Friend. Even when he was driven underground, his voice continued to be heard. The police succeeded in briefly silencing *Ami du peuple* from time to time, but never for long. Fellow journalist Jacques Hébert marveled at Marat's elusiveness: "In vain have they tried to shake heaven and earth to stop Marat from writing. In spite of the Châtelet, in spite of the bayonets, in spite of martial law, he just keeps on writing. The more they persecute him, the more papers he sells."[40]

The reasons why Marat was able to evade arrest and continue publishing were not obvious to his contemporaries. It was not an inexplicable miracle, however; it was made possible by the social context, and by certain aspects of Marat's activities that he was obliged to keep hidden from public view. The social context was the deep political radicalization that surrounded Marat with a vast multitude of active and passive supporters. He had cultivated an intelligence-gathering network of contacts and sources that kept him a step ahead of the authorities. His "eyes and ears" at the Châtelet and at City Hall were the secret of his survival. Furthermore, when Marat needed a safe haven there was no shortage of patriotic citizens willing to provide shelter for their hero. Above all, the fact that thousands of *sans-culottes* were ready and eager to take to the streets in his defense at a moment's notice made the authorities move cautiously in pursuing the People's Friend.

The deepening radicalization also explains Marat's ability to continue publishing even when forced into hiding. Despite persistent police harassment and occasional arrests, printers tended to become bolder and more willing to produce banned publications. Marat was also able to rely upon a loyal cadre of distributors who would risk arrest for selling *Ami du peuple* on the streets and bridges of Paris. The paper-sellers would sometimes be protected by groups of husky men bearing clubs.

Marat's ability to carry on with minimal interruption was not a matter of luck or karma, but of the careful planning and organization of his operations. His underground activities were by definition hidden from view, but some of the details have been preserved in the police archives. Bundles of the journal and the cash to pay for them were transmitted between Marat and the printers via several layers of intermediaries. When printers or paper-sellers were arrested and interrogated they claimed they had never seen Marat in person, and that may well have been the truth.

On October 8, 1789, at the time Marat first went into hiding, his clandestine publishing network had yet to be formed. *Ami du peuple* was suppressed for nearly a month, until a new issue appeared on November 5. In the meantime Marat hid himself in a succession of supporters' homes, beginning with a country house near Versailles. He later reported that about ten days into his first venture into the underground he was almost caught. A "traitor" had recognized him, he said, and divulged the location of his hiding place to the National Guard. A unit led by Lecointre, the captain of the Versailles National Guard, confronted him and asked who he was. "The People's Friend," Marat responded. Luckily for Marat, Lecointre happened to be a devoted reader of *Ami du peuple*. Not only was Marat not arrested, but Lecointre offered him asylum in his own home, which he accepted.[41]

Marat was determined to bring his journal back into existence, but he could not do so without returning to Paris.

He found another hideout, in Montmartre, where he remained for about two weeks. Marat was not a romantic revolutionary who thought the clandestine lifestyle was somehow ennobling. He went underground only as a last resort, not as a matter of principle. His primary objective was to get his revolutionary message out to the public, and being in hiding was a hindrance. Whenever the political conditions allowed, Marat embraced legality and resumed publishing openly.

When he decided it was safe to come out of hiding he reestablished himself in the Cordeliers district, where *Ami du peuple* had a large and loyal readership. The November 5 issue, the first since the journal's temporary suppression, came off Marat's own presses. He had for the first time set up a type shop and become his own printer, while continuing to have part of his press run produced by other shops. Although that freed him from total dependence on outside printers, it also made him more vulnerable to police raids.

### MARAT MEETS LAFAYETTE

After its reappearance on November 5, *Ami du peuple* came out daily for two weeks before it disappeared again for three weeks. A single issue appeared on December 11 but the following day Marat was arrested and his presses were confiscated, interrupting publication yet again. He was soon released, however, and the journal resumed its run on December 19. In that issue he told the remarkable tale of his arrest and detention:

> Spies, shadowing some friends who were visiting me, discovered my hideout, and last Saturday at dawn I was assailed by a detachment of 25 men, led by the vice president of the Saint-Nicolas-du Chardonnet district. My host [the person who had been hiding Marat], half dead with fear, led them to my door. I opened it in my pajamas.
>
> 'What can I do for you, gentlemen?'
>
> 'We've come to arrest you.'

'May I see your warrant? All right; I'm your man. Please allow me to get dressed.'

My papers were confiscated. I asked for a carriage and was taken to the investigations committee.

'The People's Friend has come to see you, gentlemen.'

'We're not ready for you yet.'

'How many must there be to form a tribunal?'

'Three.'

There were only two of them. I turned my back on them and took a seat in the corner. One of the gentlemen sat down near me and made small talk.

They had awakened me rather brusquely; I hadn't eaten breakfast. I accepted a cup of chocolate and continued to chat.

They were then ready to begin the proceedings. They asked me (and they knew the answers as well as I did) where I had been and why, and how long I had stayed in each place.

After the interrogation, Mr. Lafayette came in. The committee members presented me to him.

'I have been done an injustice, sir,' I said, 'by those who claim that I've attacked your principles. You have fought to break the Americans' chains; why should anyone think you would want to forge new ones for your own countrymen?'

After a rather long conversation on political subjects, I went into an adjoining room and then returned to the investigations committee.[42]

Not long afterwards, Marat was released and the charges against him were dropped. The Châtelet could not be unaware, he observed, that "today I am peacefully at home." Marat, in other words, felt secure enough to publish relatively openly—so secure, in fact, that he went to City Hall to boldly demand the return of the confiscated presses, and they were! He told his readers that "in order to serve the Nation more effectively I have made myself a printer."[43]

What was most noteworthy in Marat's account of his arrest was the dialogue with the marquis de Lafayette. Lafayette was an aristocratic military leader who, as Marat indicated in greeting him, was widely admired among French revolutionaries for the prominent role he had played as a general in the American Revolutionary War. When the Parisian National Guard was formed with him as its commander-in-chief, he became popularly known as "the hero of two continents."

It is remarkable that Lafayette did not mention the encounter with Marat in his own voluminous memoirs. If Marat had simply made it up, someone would surely have called his bluff. Lafayette most likely declined to discuss it in retrospect because it was an embarrassing political blunder on his part. He had had the incendiary journalist in his grasp; why had he let him go? Perhaps Lafayette misjudged the threat Marat represented to him and believed he could use the People's Friend to his own political advantage.

As Marat's polite demeanor toward the general indicates, Lafayette had not yet become a target of his invective. At that time his harshest polemics were aimed at Jacques Necker, whom Lafayette viewed as a political rival. Necker and Lafayette both aspired to become chief minister of state in the anticipated constitutional government. Marat no doubt owed his liberty at that moment to Lafayette's hope that *Ami du peuple*'s attacks on Necker would prove useful. Before long, however, Lafayette would come to regret his miscalculation as he himself increasingly became the focus of Marat's unrelenting denunciations.

Marat published detailed accounts of his run-ins with the law for a reason. They were intended as morality tales to show that the municipal authorities were using their powers to persecute a man whose only "crime" was his consistent devotion to the nation. It was a way to demonstrate that the new, ostensibly revolutionary regime could be as oppressive and despotic as the old one had been. "The People's Friend pursued like a common criminal by the public officials!" he exclaimed. "Who could think it possible—unless the public officials themselves are enemies of the people?"[44]

Marat's relative freedom lasted little more than a month, from December 19, 1789 until January 22, 1790, but during that period he was able to produce his daily journal without interruption. He continued to hammer away at Necker, who he called "the most adroit and dangerous prop of arbitrary power, the cruelest adversary of freedom, the solidest support of the aristocracy." He likewise attacked the mayor of Paris, Jean Sylvain Bailly, as "Necker's tool," but for the time being continued to spare Lafayette.[45]

On the last day of 1789, his journal characterized "almost everything the city government, the mayor, and the committees of the National Assembly do" as "trickery, traps, and treason."[46] Marat was no longer an unknown who could be easily ignored. On the day these words appeared in print the district committee of the Sorbonne brought criminal charges against him. On the evening of January 9 a National Guard detachment raided Marat's printshop on orders from the Châtelet, but Marat had been tipped off and had vacated the premises. In the next day's issue of *Ami du peuple* he described how he had witnessed the raid through the keyhole of an adjacent apartment, where he had taken refuge. He saw the soldiers search his printshop and confiscate the proofs of a pamphlet entitled *Denunciation of Necker* that was ready to go to press.

Marat called on the Cordeliers district and his fellow journalists to protest the raid and defend his right to publish. On January 11 he was ordered to appear before Mayor Bailly and the city council. Marat's response was a defiant letter refusing to obey and reminding them that his journal was legal. Two days later a second arrest warrant was issued and on January 15 the city council indicted Marat on charges of "incendiary writings, provoking the people to violate the sanctity of the laws ... with the intent of plunging the capital into anarchy."[47]

The Cordeliers district rose to Marat's defense by passing a series of regulations claiming jurisdiction over arrest procedures in their territory. Thus protected, Marat went ahead and published the 69-page *Denunciation of Necker*. Its message was that Necker's "heart is with the capitalists, the bankers, the speculators. He is their God and they are his apostles."[48] By this time the influence of Marat's journal had grown to become a matter of concern not only for the local authorities, but for politicians at the national level as well. National Assembly leaders denounced the Cordeliers district for protecting the subversive outlaw.

Among the leadership of the Cordeliers district was a dynamic but still virtually unknown young attorney named Georges Jacques Danton. Danton had been among Marat's most loyal supporters since the earliest appearance of *Ami du peuple*. On January 21, when Danton learned that yet another warrant for Marat's arrest had been issued, he put out a call to mobilize the district's defenses for the following day.

## THE GREAT CONFRONTATION OF JANUARY 22

Although Marat's celebrity had grown considerably in the four and a half months since the launch of his journal, by mid-January 1790 he had not yet really distinguished himself in the public mind from the large number of radical agitators who had come on the scene at about the same time. On January 22 the renown of the People's Friend took a quantum leap forward that left the others in the dust. It could not have happened without a major assist from his political enemies.

Mayor Bailly and General Lafayette joined forces in an effort to silence Marat once and for all, but all they accomplished was to make him a *cause célèbre*, and in doing so came close to starting a civil war.[49] The occasion was yet another raid on Marat's printshop, but this was no routine operation. Wanting to leave nothing to chance, Bailly had arranged for support from the National Guard. In the early morning hours of January 22, Lafayette dispatched several detachments of infantry and cavalry, complete with heavy artillery, to back up the arresting officers. Later estimates of the number of troops at the scene ranged from several hundred to a few thousand.

When the police arrived at Marat's door, however, they were stopped by Danton and told that their arrest warrant was not valid. The arrest could only be carried out legally, he said, if it bore the signatures of five Cordeliers district commissioners. Danton threatened to "sound the tocsin" if the National Guard made a move against Marat. A tocsin was an alarm bell that was traditionally used for any emergency, but in the context of the Revolution, its ringing signified a call to insurrection. He warned that the district was fully armed, including its women, an indication of the respect that the militancy of women had gained following the October Days.

A standoff ensued as police representatives went before the district assembly, then in special session, to argue their case for a legal arrest warrant. Tension escalated during two hours of turbulent debate. The National Guard troops were put on battle alert. Meanwhile, an appeal for all patriotic citizens to assemble in arms around Marat's printshop brought people from the Cordeliers and neighboring districts flooding into the area. Lafayette and the police officials insisted they would not back away from arresting Marat, but the crowd's hostility mounted and the National Guard officers could not be sure rank-and-file Guardsmen would obey if ordered to open fire on their fellow citizens.

The National Guard commanders on the scene prudently avoided provoking the crowd further, but the standoff continued throughout the entire day and into the early hours of January 23, when the police were at last allowed to enter the printshop. To nobody's surprise, Marat was long gone. Danton congratulated Plainville, the National Guard commander, on his "magnificent victory."

Marat's presses were once again seized and he was forced back into hiding, but the most significant consequences of the day's events were the boost it gave to the *sans-culottes*' confidence in the power of their militancy, and the elevation of Marat and Danton in the estimation of radicalizing public opinion. The legend of the People's Friend attained heroic proportions. An army had been sent to capture him ... and failed!

## FLIGHT TO ENGLAND

The stepped-up police repression, however, dealt Marat a temporary setback by forcing *Ami du peuple* out of existence for several months. During the month preceding the great confrontation Marat had been living in only partial clandestinity, working openly at his publicly known address during the day, but sleeping in a different secret location every night. With the intensified police pressure on him following January 22, he was forced into a fully underground existence. After a month in deep hiding he dejectedly left France and went into exile in England.

Fearing French spies, Marat hid himself from public view even in England, and little is known of his activities in exile. Continuing publication of his journal was impossible under those conditions, but he was able to produce three new pamphlets and arrange for their distribution in France. The most noteworthy of the three was the 67-page *Appeal to the Nation*, an autobiographical narrative recounting the People's Friend's battles for liberty and justice.[50]

Due to his prominent role in the attempted capture of Marat on January 22, Lafayette was instantly raised to the top of Marat's list of enemies, right alongside Necker and Bailly. In *Appeal to the Nation*, Marat lambasted Lafayette for trying to turn the National Guard into an instrument in the service of the wealthy. Another new target of his wrath was his former friend and admirer Brissot, who Marat now accused of selling himself to Bailly.

One somewhat peculiar element of Marat's writing was the frequency with which the People's Friend berated not only enemies of the people, but the people themselves. Although he expressed confidence in their revolutionary *potential*, he often bitterly assailed his readers for failing to heed his warnings. "Oh Parisians, you're nothing but children," he wrote. "You're happy to be in chains, so keep wearing them. Keep adoring the divine Necker, the heroic Lafayette, the immortal Bailly!"[51]

Marat believed the Revolution could not succeed without a strong leader able and willing to implement strong measures. He had no particular candidate to recommend for the job, but he insisted that the answer to the social crisis was to name a "supreme dictator." This dictator would not have to remain in power more than a few weeks, but during his incumbency he would be "armed with full public power and charged with punishing those who were to blame" for the nation's suffering. "A few heads chopped off now," he declared, "could rid a great nation for a long, long time of the misery of poverty and the horrors of civil war."[52]

Historians have often cited Marat's call for a dictator as evidence that he favored the establishment of a totalitarian regime. That does not seem to have been Marat's intent. The function of his proposed dictator was not to rule permanently but to remove roadblocks to the consolidation of the Revolution. Later, when his influence had reached its highest point, he would say that the Revolution needed a "chief." When accused again of advocating totalitarianism, Marat responded that he used the word "chief" to mean *leader*, not *dictator*.[53] For frequently declaring the desirability of "chopping off a few heads," Marat was accused of glorifying bloodshed. His response was an eloquent argument for the necessity of revolutionary violence. Those who failed to perceive the massacres that awaited them if the enemies of the Revolution were to triumph, Marat said, were living in a dream world.

From his London sanctuary, Marat kept a close eye on the Parisian political scene, and before long he began to detect harbingers of change for the better at home. On April 1 the release of a long list of royal "pensioners"—idle aristocrats supported by immense sums of public funds—had been greeted by widespread outrage. Marat's longstanding accusation implicating Necker in this financial support of "traitors" was vindicated. Necker tried but failed to prevent the list from being made public and was politically ruined.

Also, at about the same time, Marat's ally Danton had been elected president of the Cordeliers district by an almost unanimous vote. Then on April 27 a new political organization was formed in the Cordeliers district that Marat considered superior to the Jacobin Club as a source of revolutionary leadership. Although the word "Jacobin" has come to signify the pinnacle of French Revolution radicalism, the Club's radicalism was muted at first and only sharpened during the course of the struggle. In the first days of the Revolution, its membership consisted only of delegates to the Estates General, and even after it opened its doors to others, its membership fees were so high that only well-off gentlemen could afford to join. Given that social composition, it is not surprising that the club was dominated by a politically moderate wing. The deepening of the Revolution, however, had a profound effect on the organization, leading to a major split in July 1791 in which the moderate wing departed. The Jacobin Club then rapidly developed into the beacon of radicalism from which its historical reputation derives.

But before the Jacobins' transformation, the new group in the Cordeliers district provided revolutionary activists with an alternative organizational model. Its dues were affordable to the plebeian classes, and it welcomed all supporters of the Revolution, including women. Its formal name was the "Society of Friends of the Rights of Man and of the Citizen," but it quickly became known simply as the Cordeliers Club.

## RETURN TO PARIS

These signs of hope boosted Marat's spirits and gave him confidence that he could return and, with the Cordeliers' support, resume putting out his journal without undue risk. He was back in Paris by the second week of May 1790 and on May 18 *Ami du peuple* made its first appearance in almost four months. From that point forward the journal would appear daily with almost no interruptions for more than a year, until July 20, 1791.

There were still active warrants out for Marat's arrest, but he found he could nevertheless operate more or less in the open, at least in the daytime, at his former workplace at 39 Ancienne Comédie Street in the Cordeliers district. *Ami du peuple* boldly displayed that address as its place of publication, but it was not entirely true. Marat, who was virtually the sole writer and editor, and a skeleton crew of stalwarts who assisted him did indeed work out of offices at that address, but those who set the type, operated the presses, checked the proofs, addressed the subscription labels, toted bundles of papers to the post office, and dispatched the fluctuating corps of street vendors were now operating elsewhere. Marat had ceased to be his own printer and was secretly farming the entire press run out to a number of other printshops. If the police stopped one of them from printing *Ami du peuple*, the operation would simply move on to another.[54]

A printshop on Gît-le-Cœur Street is one that appears regularly in the police records of the time. Its proprietor was a widow Meunier, and her shop seems to have served as one of Marat's main distribution centers. The police staked it out frequently and observed men and women arriving empty-handed and leaving with bundles of papers under their arms. Although *Ami du peuple* was not the only radical periodical Mme. Meunier printed, it was the one the authorities were most concerned with. She was arrested and questioned from time to time, and the newspaper hawkers were followed, but Marat's precautions sufficed to shield him from arrest.

During daylight hours the vigilant eyes and ears of the Cordeliers section afforded Marat sufficient protection, but come nightfall he would go into hiding. Every evening he went underground—literally as well as figuratively, because he most often had to sleep in the basements of comrades and well-wishers. He changed hideouts frequently; he said he was "unable to sleep in the same bed for two nights in a row."[55] Marat's nocturnal sanctuaries were uncomfortable and probably unhealthy.[56] The subterranean dankness of Parisian basements and the inability to change clothing as often as he might have liked may well have aggravated his chronic skin disease. According to people who knew him at that time, he often wore a vinegar-soaked handkerchief around his forehead to relieve the inflammation.

Despite his poor health and less than ideal working conditions, Marat's literary output over the last four years of his life was prodigious. From the birth of *Ami du peuple* on September 12, 1789, to its final issue of July 14, 1793, its approximately 7,500 pages were filled with material mostly written and all edited by himself. On top of that were the many pamphlets, placards, and books he wrote and published during the same period.

Unsatisfied with that, however, he continuously sought further outlets for his political pronouncements. Around the end of June 1790 he made overtures to other popular journalists, proposing collaboration. To his "dear comrade in arms" Camille Desmoulins, he suggested publishing a series of articles jointly in *Ami du peuple* and Desmoulins' *Révolutions de France et de Brabant*.[57] In a new daily newspaper with a name that obviously echoed Marat's, *L'Orateur du peuple*, Louis Stanislaus Fréron opened his pages to Marat.

Marat's relationships with these and other leading journalists were clearly not characterized by sectarianism on his part. Far from seeking to stand apart from them, he dealt with those he considered honest revolutionaries not as rivals but as comrades. Desmoulins, Fréron, Audouin, Prudhomme, and Robert were among those whom Marat praised as his "dear brothers-in-arms, the patriotic journalists."[58] He did not try to portray himself, at their expense, as the only "real" revolutionary, and if he engaged in polemics with them, it was always over significant political disagreements.

## MARAT AND HIS "DEAR CAMILLE"

Marat's closest journalistic ally was Camille Desmoulins, whose personal role on the fateful day of July 14, 1789, had become legendary. The young agitator had jumped onto a table in the gardens of the Palais-Royal and galvanized an angry but unfocused crowd with his oratory. After founding their respective periodicals, Marat and Desmoulins became friends, but it was not a symmetrical relationship. Marat treated the younger man in a somewhat paternalistic manner, chiding his "dear Camille" for frivolity, to which Desmoulins would respond by telling Marat to lighten up.

Desmoulins wielded humor as a weapon against the Revolution's enemies; his account of medical reports to the National Assembly on the quality of the King's bowel movements is a classic.[59] Marat's style, by contrast, was deadly serious.

Irony and bitter sarcasm were part of his arsenal, but he told Desmoulins that their job was not to make their readers laugh— it was to make them angry. Too much jocularity, he insisted, was diverting, disarming, "frivolous."

As time passed, however, it became evident that more than mere differences in personality or style separated the two men. Substantive differences in political outlook came to the fore as they began increasingly to criticize each other in their journals. Some of Marat's polemics shed light on important aspects of his own approach to revolutionary journalism. Marat faulted Desmoulins for addressing his arguments to supporters of the royal regime in the naïve hope of convincing them to change their ways. We should be talking to the victims of oppression, not their oppressors, Marat explained, to educate and organize the *sans-culottes* to fight their enemies.

Desmoulins charged Marat with being too quick to propagate conspiracy theories on too little evidence. Marat countered that it would be irresponsible of him to do otherwise. Hesitating to call attention to a suspected plot until "judicial proof" was available would give the initiative to the conspirators. It was preferable, he told Desmoulins, to publicize too many alleged plots than too few.[60] On the other hand, Marat had made it clear that he would only print information that he knew was from a reliable source, although it was not necessary—and could often be dangerous—to identify the source. He also said he never printed information from anonymous sources because that would make him vulnerable to manipulation by the police's *agents provocateurs.*

When Marat proposed to Desmoulins in June 1790 that they jointly publish a series of articles in their journals, he wanted their focus to be on the draft constitution under consideration by the National Assembly. The document would be analyzed from the standpoint of the interests of the *sans-culottes.* He sent Desmoulins the first installment, the essence of which was summed up in its subtitle: *Very Serious Complaints of Those Who Have Nothing Against Those Who Have Everything.*[61]

Desmoulins, however, apparently did not approve of Marat's analysis because he did not print it. Instead, he reprinted one of Marat's earlier *Ami du peuple* articles, which was on a different subject entirely.[62] This incident demonstrates the crucial difference that distinguished Marat from most of the other prominent agitators of the Revolution. The single-minded objective of the People's Friend was to advance the *social* revolution in the most profound sense of the term. A revolution that toppled the monarchy or curbed the power of the aristocracy would mean little to Marat if it did not also raise the majority of the people out of abject poverty. "What will we have gained by destroying the aristocracy of nobility," he asked, "if it is simply replaced with an aristocracy of wealth?"[63]

Desmoulins and most of his fellow journalists, by contrast, were mainly focused upon getting rid of the old regime. They were happy to see the *sans-culottes* join the struggle against aristocratic privilege and royal power, but the plight of the urban poor was not their central concern. That was also true of the main left-wing political leaders, including Danton and even the most influential of them all, Maximilien Robespierre. Robespierre was the primary organizer of the political forces that would lead the Revolution to its earth-shaking climax. His social base, however, was not the great masses of the urban poor, but the substantial "middle" layer of Parisian radicals who "with remarkably few exceptions were drawn from the commercial *bourgeoisie*, the professions, or the liberal aristocracy."[64] They expected the poor to serve the interests of the Revolution, but for Marat it was the other way around: The purpose of the Revolution was to serve the interests of the poor.

The article by Marat that Desmoulins rejected was aimed at boosting the political consciousness of the Parisian poor. It was not a polemic against the reactionary aristocracy but against the *nouveaux riches* who Marat accused of exploiting the Revolution to further enrich themselves. Desmoulins, who admired the National Assembly leader Mirabeau as well as Marat, apparently had little interest in promoting a campaign of genuine class struggle.

In May and June of 1791 Marat would further differentiate himself from other prominent opinion-makers—and demonstrate his willingness to stand alone on matters of principle—by vigorously opposing a National Assembly attack on workers' rights. The interests of wageworkers, whose social weight in the Parisian population was relatively small, were routinely ignored by politicians, including those who professed themselves to be revolutionaries.[65] When the National Assembly issued the Le Chapelier laws denying the right of collective bargaining and prohibiting all associations, coalitions, or organizations of workers, Marat raised a loud protest against their injustice. The Le Chapelier laws' purpose was abundantly clear to the People's Friend: to allow employers to hold down their workers' wages.

As complex as Marat's relationship with other radical leaders was, the dialectic of his interaction with the revolutionary masses was even more so. At certain moments a call to insurrection by the People's Friend could bring them into the streets by the hundreds of thousands. More often, however, he seemed completely isolated, haranguing his readers and battling their transitory enthusiasms. Marat did not gain the influence he eventually attained by pandering to the moods of the Parisian crowd or adapting to them.

## THE FESTIVAL OF FEDERATION

A major celebration was held on July 14, 1790, to mark the first anniversary of the great uprising at the Bastille. While most revolutionary-minded Parisians greeted the planned commemoration with great excitement, Marat denounced it in advance as a "vain spectacle," placing him more than ever at odds with those he sought to influence. He made no effort to hide his contempt: "Blind citizens whom my cries of pain cannot penetrate—sleep on, on the edge of the abyss ... Wait stupidly for the death you're preparing for yourselves! Will you never cease to be victims of your own credulity?"[66]

It was nothing but a trap, Marat warned, a "celebration where your implacable enemies will swear fraternal friendship to you." On July 14, the day of the Festival, he issued a pamphlet condemning it: *The Infernal Project of the Enemies of the Revolution*.[67]

Among other concerns, Marat was wary of a proposal to place all of the National Guards throughout France under a single unified command. To most partisans of the Revolution, this sounded like an excellent idea: How could unity be objectionable? But Marat feared that given the relative weight of the Parisian National Guard, the unified command would be headed by the Revolution's nemesis, Lafayette. Marat addressed himself not only to his usual Parisian following, but also to the *fédérés*—provincial National Guardsmen—who would be converging on Paris from all over the country to attend the Festival of Federation. The People's Friend wanted to warn them that Lafayette was planning a *coup d'état* to make himself a dictator and crush the Revolution.

On July 8, with *fédérés* flooding into the city, *Ami du peuple* appealed to them to resist any orders to act against the interests of the nation, and to be prepared to turn their weapons against their officers if necessary. Fearing that his journal was not reaching enough of the provincial Guardsmen, he decided to experiment with another propaganda medium: the placard, or wall poster. In addition to their usual task of hawking *Ami du peuple*, Marat's loyal distributors also posted his placards on walls throughout Paris to warn the *fédérés* against being duped by Lafayette.

Much to Marat's dismay, his jeremiads were largely ignored and the Festival of Federation turned into a feel-good celebration of social harmony. It marked the low point in a general decline of revolutionary militancy that had been taking place throughout the spring and early summer. Marat despaired at the complacency of the people. They were behaving as if the Revolution had achieved its final victory, while he was convinced that it was in grave danger of being extinguished.

If the people were asleep, then the People's Friend would just have to shout louder. He decided that in order to shock the comatose masses out of their stupor he would have to make a major adjustment in his agitational techniques. As early as the beginning of June he had asked his readers, "Will it always be necessary to treat you like overgrown children?"

> Soon you won't open your eyes to anything but cries of alarm, of murder, of treason … How can I keep your attention? How can I keep you awake? There's only one thing left for me to do; I'll have to take your tastes into consideration and change my tone. Oh, Parisians! No matter how bizarre this will make me appear in the eyes of scholars, I won't hesitate to do it—your old friend cares only for your safety. I have to keep you from falling into the abyss.[68]

It is somewhat amusing that Marat foresaw the judgment of future historians who would cite his inflammatory rhetoric to depict him as a "madman." He announced in advance that he was going to become more shrill, more frenetic, more hysterical, more "bizarre," if that was what was necessary to rekindle the Parisians' revolutionary spirit. And that is what he did. As extreme as Marat's polemical style became, however, it never declined in political sophistication. It avoided the crude street slang, expletives, and bathroom humor utilized by other popular journalists such as Hébert and Lemaire. Nor did he fall back upon empty ultimatums or abstract "Down with the government!" sloganeering. Rather than continuously calling upon the *sans-culottes* to rise up in unfocused revolt, he chose his issues carefully.

Marat was aware, for example, of the power of the demand for universal suffrage to incite the disenfranchised Parisian poor to revolutionary action. His journal continuously hammered away against the traditional division of citizenship into "active" and "passive" categories, which was utilized to deny propertyless citizens the right to vote. When the National Assembly's constitution committee proposed to uphold that tradition by extending the franchise to wageworkers, but only those who paid a tax equivalent to three days' wages, Marat raised a howl of protest in the pages of *Ami du peuple*.[69]

## "IT'S ALL OVER FOR US!"

Marat's new shock-tactics campaign was launched on July 26, 1790, by a placard with a headline screaming "It's All Over for Us!"[70] It was destined to become the single most notorious example of Marat's extremism and violence-baiting. In it he claimed that a reliable source had just given him a document containing positive evidence of a counterrevolutionary plot to help Louis XVI flee Paris, join up with an émigré army at Metz, and launch a military assault on Paris. (Ironically, the author of the plot was none other than Marat's former employer, the comte d'Artois.)

Marat said he had sent the documentary evidence to the National Assembly, which merely sent it on to the Parisian municipal government, and neither seemed to show any interest in it. Marat charged them all with criminal laxity and denounced them as traitors. He listed a number of specific steps that he demanded be taken to foil the plot, and ended the placard with a passage designed to startle his readers into sitting up and taking notice:

> *Five or six hundred heads chopped off* would assure you peace, liberty and happiness. A false humanitarianism has restrained your arms and has prevented you from striking such blows. That will cost the lives of millions of your brothers. Let your enemies triumph for an instant and torrents of blood will flow. They'll cut your throats without mercy, they'll slit the bellies of your wives, and in order to forever extinguish your love of liberty, their bloody hands will reach into your children's entrails and rip their hearts out.[71]

As he had hoped, the placard had the effect of throwing a dynamite charge into the political discourse. The explicit call to chop off a few hundred heads shocked even Desmoulins, who pretended to believe that provocateurs had posted the placard in Marat's name to discredit him.[72] But Marat affirmed his authorship in the August 16 issue of *Ami du peuple* and said he stood by every word. For more than 200 years authors hostile to Marat have quoted these lines as evidence of his bloodthirstiness.

The storm over the wall poster lasted a month. Police, politicians, and pundits were united in their condemnations of Marat's "incendiary tract." Fourteen of his street-corner hawkers were arrested, and on July 29 the authorities ordered that Marat himself be taken into custody. Once again he made sure the police could not find him. On July 31 a National Assembly leader, Pierre Victor Malouet, denounced Marat and Desmoulins, and engineered the passing of a decree to arrest all "authors, printers, and distributors who incite the people to insurrection against the laws, to bloodshed, and to the overthrow of the Constitution."[73] Robespierre rose to the defense of Desmoulins, but no one wanted to risk association with Marat's call to chop off heads. Two days later the more progressive wing of the Assembly managed to have the decree revised so that it no longer applied to *all* authors, printers, and distributors, but only to Marat! Remaining alone under indictment, Marat responded by declaring his pride at having been singled out for attack by the traitors of the National Assembly.

At this point, Marat was being vigorously pursued by the Châtelet's police, Lafayette's National Guard, the Parisian City Hall, and the National Assembly. By mid-June, however, he had already disappeared into the underground and had his subterranean network of informants, printers, and distributors up and running. Consequently, *Ami du peuple* did not miss an issue throughout the month-long furor. But Marat's ability to operate at least partially in the open had come to an end. For the next two years he would lead a completely clandestine existence.


## A PATRIOTIC MUTINY

In August 1790 the widespread illusions about the possibility of lasting social harmony began to dissolve. A major struggle broke out in the army, pitting rank-and-file soldiers against their officers. As Marat had predicted, the people were awakening from their slumber and the country was entering into a period of revolutionary crises.

The metaphors of sleeping, dreaming, and awakening were frequent themes in Marat's polemical writing. During that month of August, in addition to the daily issues of his journal, he wrote three wall posters with titles that formed a logical sequence:

- August 9:   *We're Being Lulled to Sleep—Be on Guard!*
- August 26:  *It's a Beautiful Dream, but Beware the Awakening!*
- August 31:  *The Horrible Awakening*[74]

The People's Friend's network of information sources reached deep into the ranks of both the regular army and the National Guard. Earlier, on June 13, he had published an account of an incident that had taken place at the royal garrison at Nancy. Although it concerned a relatively minor problem, it typified the injustices the soldiers faced on a daily basis. To provide context for his readers, he described the political composition of the army:

> Everyone knows that the officers of this regiment (as of the majority of others) are almost all sworn enemies of the Revolution. Everybody also knows that the soldiers and non-coms of this regiment (as of all the others) are excellent patriots.[75]

Two months after the small incident at Nancy, a major mutiny erupted in the same garrison. The soldiers, distressed by the nonpayment of wages owed them, chose a spokesperson to present their grievance to the officers; the representative was severely flogged. Outraged by this flagrant injustice, the soldiers mutinied. Their rebellion spread to other regiments in Nancy, and the mutineers gained the support of the local National Guard and the Nancy branch of the Jacobin Club.

The mutiny rapidly became a national political issue. The majority of the National Assembly, concerned only

with maintaining discipline in the armed forces, demanded
that loyal troops be sent to suppress the rebellion by force.
Lafayette concurred.

Marat was enraged at seeing two institutions created by the
Revolution—the National Assembly and the National Guard—
taking the side of the Revolution's worst enemies. Earlier, on
August 6, when Lafayette had proposed a bill in the National
Assembly that would have denied the right of free assembly to
soldiers and imposed harsh punishments on violators, Marat's
response in *Ami du peuple* was to advise soldiers to assert the
right to elect their officers. If their present officers dared resist
that reasonable measure, he added, the soldiers should kill them.

With the mutiny threatening to spread beyond Nancy,
Lafayette demanded that "a great blow must be struck." On
August 16 the National Assembly voted their approval, and
Lafayette transmitted the order to the military commander
of the region, the marquis de Bouillé. Bouillé happened to be
Lafayette's cousin. On August 20 the most influential leader of
the National Assembly, the comte de Mirabeau, proposed that
the army be purged so it could be rebuilt on the basis of absolute
obedience to officers. Marat responded in print on August 22
that the army should indeed be purged—not its ranks, but its
officer corps. On top of that, he called for hanging 800 of the
National Assembly deputies with Mirabeau at their head, and
burning the ministers of state at the stake in the palace gardens.[76]

After making these hair-raising proposals, he dared Malouet
to call him an assassin again. Malouet obliged, and demanded
that Marat and anyone associated with his journal be arrested.
In response, Marat ridiculed Malouet for taking what he had
written at face value. It should have been obvious, he said, that
his suggestion to hang deputies and roast state officials was a
rhetorical device—a *reductio ad absurdum*—to call attention
to the outrageousness of what was being done to the soldiers
at Nancy.[77]

By August 26, when Marat's "Beautiful Dream" placard
appeared on the walls of Paris, the Nancy mutiny had by
all appearances been peacefully concluded. Marat, however,

suspected that the lull was temporary. The authorities were playing for time, he warned, as they gathered troops from elsewhere for an all-out assault against the mutinous soldiers. His suspicions proved to be well-founded. General Bouillé was en route to Nancy with his troops and the Metz National Guard, and on August 31 he launched an attack. The Nancy regiments were defeated in a fierce battle that left large numbers of casualties on both sides. Afterwards Bouillé had dozens of soldiers hanged for their role in the mutiny. The Nancy National Guard was dissolved and the local Jacobin Club was forced to disband.

The third of Marat's trilogy of placards, *The Horrible Awakening*, appeared on that very same day. Its timing was remarkable, because news reports immediately began to confirm the accuracy of Marat's grim warnings:

> Apathetic citizens! Are you going to watch in silence as your brothers are crushed? Will you sit by as legions of assassins slit their throats? The soldiers of the Nancy garrison are innocent, they are oppressed, they are resisting tyranny.[78]

The bloodbath at Nancy, ordered by the National Assembly and executed by Lafayette's cousin, did lead to a "horrible awakening" in Paris, as Marat had predicted. Other popular journalists joined him in expressing their outrage and for the first time since the October Days of the previous year, their calls for action were heeded. On September 2 and 3 huge demonstrations, bordering on insurrection. rocked the city. Order was restored only when Necker, whose earlier popularity had vanished, was forced from office in disgrace.

At the same time, the National Assembly, at the behest of Mirabeau and Lafayette, voted to congratulate Bouillé for his "firmness" in crushing the mutiny. Only a small minority of the deputies, led by Robespierre, opposed the motion. Lafayette ordered the Parisian National Guard to celebrate Bouillé's victory and mourn his casualties. The King personally voiced his strong endorsement of Bouillé's action.

The French Revolution had passed another point of no return. A line of blood had been drawn and sides had been chosen. Mirabeau, Lafayette, the National Assembly majority, and Louis XVI had lined up on the side of social order. On the other side— the side of social justice—stood Marat, Robespierre, and the vast majority of Parisians, who perceived the soldiers of Nancy as victims of unjust repression. It was no longer possible to admire both Mirabeau and Marat, and Marat's prediction that Lafayette would soon be exposed as a traitor and forced to flee began to seem less unreasonable to many Parisians.

The Nancy events gave a great boost to Marat's reputation as a prophet. He had foreseen the massacre long before it came to pass, and his vision of the "horrible awakening" had been posted on the walls on the very day it happened. "Oh People's Friend! Oh Cassandra Marat!" Desmoulins exclaimed. "How right you were when you warned that it was all over for us!"[79] He later added, "When I consider how many of the things [Marat] predicted have come to pass, I am inclined to buy his almanacs."[80]

The illusions of social unity had been greatly weakened by the Nancy massacre but had not completely dissipated. The King remained on his throne, the National Assembly continued to legislate, and Lafayette retained his positions of authority in the army and the National Guard. An uneasy calm would prevail for almost another year, until June 1791 when Louis XVI would be caught trying to flee France.

*Ami du peuple* continued to appear daily, but with its political stance shifted a bit more toward republicanism.[81] For the first time, Marat began to assail the King directly, saying he was "covered with the blood of the patriots of Nancy."[82] For the moment, however, he dismissed the idea of replacing the monarchy with a republic as impracticable, given "the degradation and vileness of henchmen of the old regime." He feared that "a federated republic would rapidly degenerate into an oligarchy" that would end up in the hands of Mirabeau and Lafayette. A King was still necessary, Marat concluded, and "taking everything into consideration," there was no choice for the job other than Louis XVI.[83]

Although social peace was maintained in the months following the events at Nancy, Marat's influence continued to rise among the politically active. He had already gained admiration as a romantic hero for his exploits in defeating the constant efforts of the police to arrest him. Now, however, the People's Friend was also increasingly perceived as a political strategist who could be looked to for guidance.

## FATHERING THE FRATERNAL SOCIETIES

Marat seems to have given little thought to the problems of political organization until mid-January 1791, when he published a proposal for the formation of political clubs.[84] What he had in mind was cadre organizations that could unite and coordinate the efforts of the most dedicated revolutionary activists. The members of such groups could join their section assemblies and work to create revolutionary majorities in them. If they could create a solid political base in the sections, the revolutionary clubs could then win control of the Paris Commune and the National Assembly.

Marat hoped that forming such revolutionary groups would lead toward the creation of a revolutionary party that could challenge the Mirabeaus, Lafayettes, and Baillys for the political leadership of the Revolution. Over the next few months a number of grassroots organizations of the kind he proposed came into being, leading Fréron to call Marat "the father of the fraternal societies." In May 1791 they took the next step by joining together in a federation and electing a central committee.

No doubt some of these nuclei of revolutionary organizations did come into being as a result of the encouragement and publicity Marat gave them, but some had already been formed prior to his call. Whether or not the fraternal-society movement owed its existence to Marat, however, it is significant that he was widely perceived to have "fathered" them.

## THE REVOLUTION DEEPENS

The political situation in Paris was shifting in Marat's favor. On February 27, 1791, a letter appeared in *Ami du peuple* that touched off a firestorm of anguish and protests. One of Marat's correspondents reported that Lafayette had placed a large order with weapons manufacturers. This, Marat charged, was evidence of a plot to massacre Parisians and to allow the King to flee.[85]

The National Assembly leaders could not ignore the uproar that ensued. They did not deny the weapons order, but explained it as a routine purchase to supply arms to the National Guard. Some sections of the Parisian National Guard, however, were unconvinced, and decided to take action on their own. A widespread rumor pointed to the Château de Vincennes as the place where the counterrevolutionaries were storing their weapons. On February 28 battalions of Guardsmen from the faubourg Saint-Antoine, one of the heavily populated *sans-culottes* neighborhoods, assembled en masse at the castle and proceeded to tear down one of its towers. Lafayette arrived on the scene and ordered them to cease and desist, but they ignored him. The importance of this incident cannot be overstated: It represented a significant rupture in the National Guard. A large part of it was no longer under Lafayette's command.

Marat's growing influence was further evidenced a few days later at the Jacobin Club. The club's secretary, Voidel, was a municipal police official, and in that capacity he had signed a warrant for Marat's arrest. At a general meeting of the club, many members angrily denounced Voidel for breaching the solidarity of the patriotic movement. His attempt to defend himself sparked a debate that revealed a great deal of support for Marat among the Jacobins. A significant minority actually shared Marat's political views, and most of the others defended his right to publish freely.[86] Even Charles Lameth, the leader of the moderate faction that was soon to split from the Jacobins, protested Voidel's action.

Despite these harbingers of change that should have encouraged Marat, he was far from satisfied. He continued to bemoan what he perceived as widespread apathy. Even the death of Mirabeau on April 2 failed to lift his spirits. To the contrary, the public outpouring of grief over the National Assembly leader's passing—especially lamentations expressed in Desmoulins' and Hébert's journals—reinforced his pessimism. Marat, who insisted on calling Mirabeau by his family name, Riquetti, once again was swimming against the tide when he exclaimed, "People, thank the gods—your most formidable enemy has fallen ... Riquetti is no more ... Save your tears for the honest men who defend you."[87] He also used the occasion to accuse the late "Riquetti" of having secretly been on the King's payroll. When that charge was later proven true, the legend of Marat's prophetic powers grew ever larger.[88]

Within two weeks of Mirabeau's death, however, new challenges arose to shake Marat out of his depression and resurrect his fighting spirit. He and other agitators had long warned of a plot to sneak Louis XVI and his family out of France, which would prompt counterrevolutionary émigrés and their Austrian allies to launch a military onslaught against Paris. An announcement that the royal family would make a trip to St. Cloud, outside the city, to celebrate Easter was met with widespread suspicion. On April 18, at the time they were scheduled to leave, a large multitude gathered at the palace to block the royal carriages' departure. Lafayette ordered the National Guard to disperse the crowd and allow the carriages to proceed, but once again the Guardsmen defied him and ignored his command.

The Easter plans for St. Cloud were cancelled, the royal family stayed in Paris, and on April 21 a mortified Lafayette announced his resignation as National Guard commander. The following day, however, his allies talked him into resuming his command. In Marat's eyes, this was a triple victory: The people had heeded his warnings, had stood up against Lafayette, and had thwarted a counterrevolutionary conspiracy. He thought it naïve to believe that the danger had passed, however, and continued to warn of further attempts to spirit the royal family out of France.

## THE FLIGHT TO VARENNES

Following the St. Cloud incident, Marat's calls for vigilance intensified. On June 6 he made his warning more specific than ever. His sources, he said, had discovered that the long-anticipated plot was to be put into action on June 18. That day passed without incident, but on June 21 *Ami du peuple* declared, "The royal family is only waiting for Paris to go to bed before taking flight."[89] As that issue was coming off the presses on the night of June 20, 1791, an ordinary-looking carriage with the King and his family hidden inside passed through the palace gates and headed for the border.

The royal fugitives nearly made good their escape, but they were stopped in the small town of Varennes. The peculiar entourage attracted the attention of local patriots, one of whom recognized the King despite his disguise. The carriage and its occupants were placed under armed guard and escorted back to Paris. The organizer of the failed conspiracy was the general who had brutally suppressed the Nancy mutiny: Lafayette's cousin, Bouillé.

Assuming the escape would be successful, the King had unwisely left behind a manifesto declaring his intentions. After that became public, he could no longer feign good will toward the Revolution. Lafayette and the National Assembly leaders had also been badly compromised. Attempting to hide their involvement, they put forward the story that the King had not tried to escape, but had been kidnapped! They tried to take the heat off themselves by scapegoating a few unpopular members of the royal court. Hardly anyone was taken in by this absurdity, however.

From that point forward, Marat referred to the King only by his civil name, Louis Capet, and branded him a traitor who deserved to be executed.[90] The June 22 issue of *Ami du peuple* reported on the attempted escape and proposed a revolutionary program to resolve the political crisis. The revelation of the monarch's untrustworthiness had left a power vacuum at the center of the social order.

Marat continued to believe that no society could survive without a strong central authority, so to replace the discredited King he again floated the idea of a tribunate, or temporary dictatorship. Without explicitly volunteering himself for the job, he made it clear that if called upon, the People's Friend would not shirk his duty. Although the proposal for a revolutionary dictatorship met with little immediate response, Marat's influence had grown to the point that his voice could not be ignored.

Many agreed with Hébert when he hailed "Marat, the prophet Marat."[91] While many agitators had suspected the plot, none had more accurately predicted it. It was not occult powers that gave Marat the ability to foresee such events, however, but his underground network of informants, which undoubtedly included sympathetic servants within the palace walls.

## HOW DID HE DO IT?

In less than two years, from Bastille Day to the Night of Varennes, Marat had transformed himself from a virtual nonentity into a potent factor affecting the course of the Revolution. What unique qualities or circumstances made him stand out from such popular agitators of the Revolution as Brissot, Gorsas, Desmoulins, Carra, Loustalot, Hébert, Bonneville, Fréron, and many others? Let us count the ways.

First and most important, Marat went beyond the call for political equality and raised the banner of social equality. He differentiated his voice from the others by persistently and loudly defending the interests of the oppressed majority.

Second, he set himself apart by his implacable opposition to the constituted authorities—not only the authorities left over from the old regime, but those who represented the new, ostensibly "revolutionary" regime as well.

Third, he demonstrated a great deal of political courage in his willingness to stand alone and "swim against the current."

Fourth, he earned a reputation as a prophet because his distinct political perspective encouraged him to see things that most of his contemporaries resisted seeing—the machinations, for example, that determined the political trajectories of Necker, Mirabeau, Lafayette, and Louis XVI.

Fifth, his refusal to back down in the face of police repression, and his ability to portray himself as an unjustly persecuted patriot, won him widespread sympathy and respect.

Sixth, he attracted the support of thousands of enthusiastic activists who were willing to come physically to his defense when necessary.

And finally, he created an underground organization of information sources, printers, and distributors that prevented his voice from being silenced.

Taken together with the sheer energy he exhibited, these constitute a sufficient explanation of Marat's rise to prominence in the context of a revolutionary situation. The essential distinction, from which all the rest flowed, was his strategic orientation of fighting for social equality.

# 4

# From the Champ de Mars Massacre to the September Massacres

## July 1791 to September 1792

Louis XVI's failed attempt to flee revolutionary Paris dramatically altered the political landscape. The monarchy lost all credibility and its days appeared to be numbered. Meanwhile, Marat's popularity skyrocketed.

One might expect Marat to have been elated, but he was not. He was pleased that naïve illusions of peaceful social reconciliation had at last been demolished, but his assessment of the general political situation left him as depressed as ever. In his view, the people had not yet fully awakened, but were sleepwalking, wandering in confusion, far, far from achieving the political clarity that would be necessary to consolidate the Revolution. He would remain gloomy for yet another year, until August 1792 when another great insurrection would at last transform revolutionary potential into revolutionary reality.

### THE CHAMP DE MARS MASSACRE

The shocking revelation that the King had conspired against the Revolution prompted widespread demands to strip him of his powers. Illness during the first weeks of July 1791 hampered Marat's ability to participate in organizing the movement, although the uninterrupted appearance of *Ami du peuple* kept his opinions before the public. Meanwhile, his Cordeliers Club allies took the lead in issuing a call for a mass mobilization on July 17 at the Champ de Mars (where the Eiffel Tower stands today).

The plan was to construct a large platform to be called the "Altar of the Nation" in the middle of the open field where throngs of demonstrators could converge to sign a protest petition. The petition that was drawn up for the event called for the ouster of Louis XVI, but did not demand the abolition of the monarchy. As people began to stream into the Champ de Mars on the morning of July 17, however, a nasty confrontation developed when two men were discovered hiding under the Altar of the Nation. Some historians have speculated that they may have been hapless voyeurs hoping for a peek up the ladies' skirts, but an aroused crowd believed them to be government spies and killed them on the spot. In response, Mayor Bailly declared martial law and called upon Lafayette's National Guard to disperse the demonstrators.

Meanwhile, tens of thousands of people had continued to enter the Champ de Mars, unaware of the earlier disturbance and the order to disperse. It was a lovely summer day. Families had brought their children and the mood was festive. Suddenly National Guardsmen opened fire on them, killing about 50 and wounding many more.

Champ de Mars Massacre: Lafayette orders his troops to fire on demonstrators. ("Lafayette au Champ de Mars, ordonne de tirer sur le peuple," drawn by Ary Scheffer, engraved by Victor Florence Pollet)

The authorities succeeded in driving the crowd from the field, but the episode immediately entered the annals of history as the Champ de Mars Massacre. It represented another watershed event—the first time the new "revolutionary" regime had turned its guns against the people. With Bailly and Lafayette widely perceived as responsible for the slaughter of peaceful demonstrators, Marat's denunciations of the two moved from the radical fringe to the mainstream. Bailly's tenure as mayor would last only two more months and Lafayette's as National Guard commander would end shortly thereafter.

Marat was unrestrained in condemning the perpetrators of the massacre. "If only the People's Friend could rally two thousand determined men," he raged, he would lead them to rip Lafayette's heart out, burn down the royal palace with the King and his ministers inside, and impale the National Assembly deputies in their seats.[1] That rant resulted in the arrest of the printer who printed it, but Marat himself was as usual able to avoid capture. Other printers were sufficiently intimidated, however, to make publication of *Ami du peuple* difficult; only two issues would appear over the following two weeks.

If Marat had expected the Champ de Mars Massacre to trigger an immediate upsurge in the fighting spirit of the people, he was disappointed. The repression may not have succeeded in intimidating the Parisian public but it certainly left it in a daze of confusion and demoralization. Revolutionary ardor declined and social peace returned, but the tranquility was deceptive. Beneath the surface, a sullen anger festered and spread.

By September Marat's despair had intensified, and he put it on public view in the pages of *Ami du peuple*. "The People's Friend," he declared in the September 8 issue, "is ready to renounce the foolish enterprise of sacrificing himself for the public welfare."[2] As if deteriorating health, mounting financial difficulties, and the depressing political situation were not enough, Marat had also been drawn into a lurid domestic scandal. His underground existence obliged him to frequently change hiding places, one of which had been at the residence of a Monsieur Maquet. Maquet had a housekeeper, Mademoiselle Fouaisse, who also happened to be his mistress.

One day, returning from a business trip, Maquet discovered that Marat and Mlle. Fouaisse were gone and some of his furniture was missing. Maquet publicly accused Marat of stealing his wife and his furniture, and brought criminal charges against him. Scandal-mongering journalists gave the allegations wide circulation, and Marat's enemies sought to use them to damage him. One of Maquet's friends denounced Marat at the Jacobin Club.

Marat responded to the charges in *Ami du peuple*. First of all, he explained, Mlle. Fouaisse was not Maquet's wife, but a servant whom he had kept in virtual slavery. Furthermore, he had witnessed Maquet physically abusing her. The young woman, a good patriot, had asked the People's Friend for guidance, and he advised her to liberate herself immediately. She did so and took with her certain pieces of furniture that she considered to be her own.[3] This rejoinder must have embarrassed Maquet into silence, because the scandal simply faded away, and seems not to have caused lasting damage to Marat's reputation for moral probity.

In the short term, however, the incident compromised Marat's security by putting a spotlight on the methods he used to hide himself. With his cover blown, he said, he had no choice but to go into exile.[4] On September 21 he published a "Final Farewell of the People's Friend to the Nation" that declared he had given up hope for France and had departed for England the previous week.[5] He had arranged with Cordeliers comrades for the continued publication of *Ami du peuple*, and the next three issues were datelined Clermont, Breteuil, and Amiens as he headed toward the coast.[6]

But a week later he was back in Paris, relating a peculiar cloak-and-dagger story in his September 27 issue. He said that en route to England he had become aware of some suspicious characters trailing him whom he feared might be assassins. They almost nabbed him in Beauvais, but he got away and then decided to return to Paris.[7] The truth of this mysterious episode is impossible to ascertain. He may have actually been in Clermont, Breteuil, Amiens and various other places as he claimed, or he may never have left Paris at all. The whole story could well have been a misdirection maneuver to deceive the police into looking for him elsewhere.

## THE LEGISLATIVE ASSEMBLY

Wherever Marat had been during the previous two weeks, when he officially resurfaced in Paris at the end of September the Revolution was entering a new phase. On October 1 a new parliamentary body, the Legislative Assembly, made its debut. The National Assembly had fulfilled its original mandate of producing a new constitution for France and, after calling elections for the new legislature, dissolved itself. The new political arrangements included a role for Louis XVI, who would be allowed to remain King if he would swear allegiance to the new constitution. With that, France would officially become a constitutional monarchy.

The politicians of the National Assembly, collectively tainted by their involvement in the debacle of the flight to Varennes, had to concede that the new Legislative Assembly would be entirely made up of people other than themselves. All members of the National Assembly were explicitly barred as candidates for the Legislative Assembly. That gave Marat a measure of hope that the new legislative body might be an improvement over its predecessor, which he had utterly loathed.

Marat had been nominated as a candidate for the Legislative Assembly, but despite the powerful impact of his journalism on certain occasions, in September 1791 his chances of being elected were virtually nil. His name was listed on only a single ballot, on which only two of the 733 electors voted for him.[8] Marat's lack of electoral appeal was not a function of his popularity, but of the class bias of the electoral system. Only "active citizens," as defined by a property qualification, were eligible to vote, which excluded the poorest third of the Parisian population.

The elections, reflecting a rise in republicanism after the King's escape attempt, produced a legislative body with a left wing significantly larger than the one Robespierre had led in the National Assembly. The most influential left-wing leader in the Legislative Assembly, however, was Marat's former friend Brissot, whom he had since come to regard as a corrupt and unprincipled scoundrel. In Marat's eyes, one Robespierre was worth more than a hundred Brissots. When in its third session the Legislative Assembly ratified the constitution produced by the National Assembly, Marat concluded that "the new deputies are worth no more than the old ones."[9]

Brissot's faction at first dominated the Legislative Assembly's left wing. Known alternatively as the "Brissotins" and the "Girondins" (because several of its other leaders represented the Gironde department of southwestern France), within the course of a few months they had become its *right* wing. As one historian observed, they started out as stalwart republicans but soon became "alarmed at the social consequences of their own actions" and "drew back in defence of the monarchy."[10]

In March 1792 the Brissotins were appointed by the King to head the government. Marat denounced the new ministry as worse than its predecessors:

> Never did our former tyrants give us as much cause for complaint as our own barbarous delegates are giving us today ... We are farther from liberty than ever. Not only are we slaves; we're slaves legally ... Take a look at the 'theater of State'—the decorations have changed, but the same actors are there, and the same masks and the same plots.[11]

## THE DRIVE TOWARD WAR

Although Louis XVI remained on the throne, monarchists within France and throughout Europe were infuriated by the humiliation to which he and his family had been subjected after his capture at Varennes. Believing he was being held as a virtual prisoner in his Parisian palace, they determined to step up efforts to "rescue" him. In August 1791 the rulers of Austria and Prussia met and issued a call for other European monarchs to join them in a military alliance against the French Revolution. Their Declaration of Pillnitz, though diplomatically formulated, was transparent enough to be perceived by French patriots as a mortal threat. War appeared to be inevitable.

Brissot and his colleagues, as the leaders of the Legislative Assembly, responded to the challenge with radically revolutionary defiance. Revolutionary France, they proclaimed, should immediately declare war against the major European powers. To simply wait for their enemies to carry out their threats of aggression would be suicidal.

The Brissotins' proclamation was an inspirational call for international revolutionary solidarity—an appeal not only to defend the Revolution in France, but to *extend* it throughout Europe. It urged oppressed people everywhere to rise up in arms against their oppressors and promised that France's revolutionary army would be there to support them.

The call for a French-led war of liberation against the crowned heads of Europe was greeted in Paris with widespread jubilation. The *sans-culottes* were suddenly re-energized. Hébert's *Père Duchesne* spoke for almost all revolutionary-minded patriots in expressing enthusiasm for the proposed revolutionary crusade. But amidst the chorus of joyous hosannas there was one loud, discordant note. Marat, too, might have been expected to welcome a call to revolutionary war, but he did not. From the moment the Brissotins launched their prowar campaign, Marat denounced it with all the energy he could muster.[12] Brissot, he thundered, was a traitor for advocating a war that could only lead the Revolution to disaster.[13]

It was the height of absurdity, Marat believed, to think that a war of liberation could be led by aristocratic generals who passionately hated the Revolution. For one example, consider Bouillé, who had massacred the patriotic soldiers at Nancy. Bouillé, it was true, was no longer on the scene, because he had fled the country after his attempt to engineer the King's escape ended in the debacle at Varennes. But who had replaced Bouillé?

His cousin, Lafayette! The same Lafayette so discredited by the Champ de Mars Massacre that he had to give up his command of the Parisian National Guard was nonetheless appointed leader of one of France's four main armies.

Marat was convinced that Lafayette and his ilk would deliberately sabotage the war effort as a way to undermine the Revolution. They would send patriotic soldiers into battle, figuratively speaking, with their hands tied behind their backs. And if the generals' perfidy succeeded in handing victory to the aristocratic émigrés, they would then all march on Paris, slaughter its inhabitants, and reestablish the autocratic monarchy. No wonder the Brissotins' war-mongering had been so warmly received by the most reactionary aristocrats and the royal court!

When reinstated in September, Louis XVI had publicly embraced the constitution, but privately he was far from reconciled to his role as constitutional monarch. He and his generals were advocating a war that they had every intention of losing. Marat smelled a conspiracy in the King's appointment of the saber-rattling Brissotins as his top ministers.

Marat perceived Brissot's ultraleft demagogy as endangering the Revolution by diverting the people's attention toward external enemies and away from the "traitors" at home. It perverted the honest patriotism of the *sans-culottes* into a reactionary form of aggressive nationalism.

The People's Friend and the moods of the people were in direct opposition on this issue. Marat's lonely stance provides insight into two qualities that were essential to his development into an effective revolutionary leader. First, the clarity and foresight of his analysis reveal his exceptional capability as a revolutionary strategist. In contrast with most of his contemporaries, his outlook was not derived from momentary enthusiasms, wishful thinking, or symbolic posturing, but was based on political and material realities. Second, his immunity to the popular war fever is evidence of an ability to resist the temptations of political opportunism.

Throughout the month of November, as circulation of *Ami du peuple* declined sharply, Marat once again seemed to grow discouraged. In December, however, his isolation on the war issue began to ease as Robespierre, for much the same reasons as Marat, also declared opposition to the Brissotins' bellicosity. Danton and other Cordeliers Club militants followed suit. Nevertheless, on December 14 Marat issued yet another "final farewell," and after its December 15 issue *Ami du peuple* did not appear again for four months.[14]

### A TWO-MONTH DISAPPEARANCE

Marat's on-again, off-again retirements are an indication that he was on a rather active emotional rollercoaster. That his ups and downs were perfectly synchronized with the rises and falls of the mass movement, however, suggests that his depression was not fundamentally a psychological problem. His periodic retreats were probably to some degree prompted by sheer physical exhaustion. The amount of energy required to publish *Ami du peuple* on a daily basis must have been draining, especially given the fragile state of his health.

His earlier "retirement" in September had lasted only two weeks. This time he disappeared from public view for two months, from late December 1791 through the end of February 1792. He so successfully covered his tracks that virtually nothing is known about where he was or what he was doing. There is no evidence to corroborate his claim to have been in England, but there is no reason to doubt it, either. Wherever he was, it can be inferred that he was busy with some major editorial projects for which he was seeking publishers as soon as he reappeared in Paris. One was to collect his articles from *Ami du peuple* and publish them in two 400-page volumes under the title *The School for Citizens*.

His two-month absence had evidently not been a retirement, but a period of reflection and reorientation that led him to take a longer view of the Revolution's prospects. Instead of expecting an imminent uprising, for which a daily agitational journal was an appropriate tool, his renewed perspective pointed toward a more prolonged struggle. That would be better served by more comprehensive works, such as *School for Citizens*, to educate the people politically and prepare them for revolutionary opportunities in the future.

The ambitious *School for Citizens* project would never be realized, but Marat put a great deal of effort into promoting it. He asked the Cordeliers Club for help, and their response was ardently supportive. On March 12 the Club appointed a special committee to promote *School for Citizens* to the fraternal societies and other revolutionary-minded organizations, not only in Paris but throughout France. More significant, however, was a motion the Club passed on April 5 urging Marat to resume publication of *Ami du peuple*, lamenting its absence as "a real public calamity."[15]

Marat responded. *Ami du peuple* started up again on April 12, 1792, and for all practical purposes served as the primary organ of the Cordeliers Club. The timing could hardly have been better. Marat's journal made its reappearance just one week before the war question—still at the center of public discourse—would cease to be an abstraction. On April 20 France declared war against Austria.


## SIMONNE ÉVRARD


Marat's decision to return to revolutionary journalism in April 1792 was also influenced by a remarkable woman he had met. Sometime in 1790 he had been introduced to the Évrard sisters, Catherine, Étiennette, and Simonne—working girls from Bourgogne who had moved to Paris to find jobs. Catherine's husband-to-be was a typographer who had set type for *Ami du peuple* and knew Marat personally. Through this connection Marat came to know the Évrard sisters, all three of whom were fervent partisans of the Revolution. He asked for their help in eluding the police and was invited to stay at the residence they shared at 243 St. Honoré Street.

One of the sisters, Simonne, became Marat's lover and, though without benefit of clergy or civil ceremony, his wife. Their relationship would last until Marat's death; following his assassination she would be known as "the widow Marat." After 31 years of steadfastly defending the memory of the People's Friend through the difficult times of the Thermidorian reaction, the Napoleonic Empire, and the Bourbon Restoration, she died in poverty in 1824.

When Marat met Simonne he was 47 and she was 26. Her first attraction was not to Jean Paul Marat but to the celebrated People's Friend. Their relationship grew out of close political collaboration. The rebirth of *Ami du peuple* in April 1792 would most likely not have been possible without the modest but essential financial support provided by her savings and wages.

## MARAT MEETS ROBESPIERRE

The two luminaries of the French Revolution's radical phase most familiar both to their peers and to posterity were Marat and Maximilien Robespierre. Strange as it may seem in retrospect, the two men met face to face on only one occasion, although they certainly knew each other well by reputation. Both later wrote of their sole encounter, but neither said exactly when it took place. It is clear that the meeting occurred during the latter stages of the debate on the war question, which would place it between Marat's reappearance in Paris in early 1792 and April 20, when the war actually began.

Robespierre and Marat by that time were on the same side of the debate, and both had been subjected to harsh political attacks by Brissot and his allies. The Brissotin ministry tried to tarnish Robespierre's reputation in the eyes of moderate Assembly deputies by alleging a secret bond between him and the incendiary People's Friend. They claimed that Robespierre was financing— perhaps even writing—Marat's violence-laced antiwar rants, and that Marat's calls for a dictator had Robespierre in mind.

Marat was indignant at the implication that he was simply a mouthpiece for Robespierre, and responded at length in *Ami du peuple*. His account of their relationship makes clear that although he was in close agreement with Robespierre on many key issues, their respective approaches to revolutionary politics were far from identical:

For those citizens who are too little enlightened to sense the absurdity of this accusation, I declare that not only does Robespierre not control my pen ... but that I have never received so much as a note from him; that I have never had any direct or indirect relations with him whatsoever; that I have only seen him once in my entire life...

The first words that Robespierre addressed to me were a reproach for having partially destroyed my journal's immense revolutionary influence by dipping my pen in the blood of the enemies of freedom, by speaking of hangmen's nooses and daggers.

'Listen,' I told him straight off, 'my journal's influence didn't come from methodical analyses of the despicable decrees of the National Assembly. It came from the horrific scandal it spread through the public by unmasking the conspiracies against public liberty that are continuously hatched by the nation's enemies—including the monarch, the legislators, and the other authorities—and by not beating around the bush about it! It came from *audacity* ... from the outpouring of my soul, from the enthusiasm of my heart, from my violent denunciations of oppression, from my impetuous outbursts against the oppressors ... You can be sure that after the massacre at the Champ de Mars, if I could have found 2,000 men who shared my feelings I would have led them to execute the general [Lafayette] in the midst of his battalions of brigands, burn the despot in his palace, and impale our atrocious representatives in their seats, just as I said I would at the time.'

Robespierre listened to me, frightened; his face turned pale and he kept silent for a while. That conversation confirmed me in the opinion I had always had of him; that in him were combined the intelligence of a wise senator, the integrity of a genuinely good man, and the zeal of a true patriot, but that he lacked both the outlook and the audacity to become a real national leader.[16]

Robespierre's comments on their one encounter corroborate Marat's account in its essentials:

> I told him ... that he himself had placed an obstacle to the good that the useful truths developed in his writings could accomplish. By insisting on dwelling upon certain absurd and violent proposals, he had disgusted the friends of liberty as much as the partisans of the aristocracy. But he defended his opinions and I persisted in mine.[17]

As a politician, Robespierre was of course afraid that Marat's violent diatribes would drive away potential allies, but his concern was not merely about political expediency. The disgust he expressed at Marat's calls to physically liquidate the Revolution's internal enemies seems to have been genuine. Ironically, less than two years later Robespierre himself would be carrying out just such a program of extermination—the Terror—and defending it as necessary for the survival of the Revolution.

In spite of great differences in temperament, Marat and Robespierre continued to respect each other. More importantly, they were solidly in agreement on the two major issues of the day: Both favored abolishing the monarchy and both were opposed to France launching a preemptive war.

By the time Marat resumed publishing *Ami du peuple* on April 12, 1792, the war issue had deeply polarized the Jacobin Club, which almost from the beginning of the Revolution had functioned as a virtual center of government. Political decisions were often hashed out at the Jacobin Club before being ratified by official governmental bodies. Robespierre headed the antiwar faction, but it represented the minority within the Club. The prowar faction led by Brissot enjoyed the considerable advantage of ministerial power. On March 15 the King had appointed Brissot's colleagues Roland, Dumouriez, Servan, and Clavière to manage the affairs of state.

Dumouriez, the Minister of Foreign Affairs as well as a top general, frequently expressed his devotion to France and to the Revolution at the Jacobin Club podium. The April 13 issue of *Ami du peuple* credited Dumouriez with "the appearance of an excellent patriot," but expressed reservations about his roles as military commander and minister of state. "Even if he were an angel," Marat wrote, "I would continue to say again and again that the first duty of all good citizens is to remain vigilant."[18] Before long the People's Friend would be directly accusing Dumouriez of treasonous intentions, and the denunciations would prove to be accurate.


## THE WAR BEGINS

On April 19 Marat's journal once again warned that only the Revolution's worst enemies wanted to see France engage in a ruinous foreign war. The royalists would sabotage it at every opportunity. Lafayette or one of his fellow generals would use it as a pretext for imposing a military dictatorship. The expense would destroy the national economy and push the poor to the brink of starvation. But far worse than the monetary cost would be the human cost, measured in the numbers of young revolutionaries who would lose their lives.

Marat's vision of how the war would unfold did not assume that the French armies would be totally defeated. His forecast was sober and prescient:

> However valiant the defenders of our liberty may be, it doesn't take a genius to predict that our armies will be crushed in their first campaign. I concede that the second might be less disastrous and that the third might even end in victory ... But to win a decisive victory over our enemies, a long and disastrous war would be necessary.[19]

The day after this article appeared the war was launched by a French attack on the Austrian Netherlands. As Marat had foreseen, the first campaigns ended in abysmal failure. On the other hand, his predictions that the French armies would get better with time and that the whole process would be "long and disastrous" were also borne out. The war would continue, off and on, for more than 20 years, until Bonaparte's final defeat at Waterloo.

The April 20 declaration of war no doubt increased the pressure to rally behind the patriotic crusade, but Marat responded by stepping up his denunciations, even going so far as asserting that French losses would be *preferable* to victories. "If we're lucky," he wrote, "our troops will be often beaten but never completely defeated. There's a real danger that one of our own generals might win a victory and, manipulating the drunken joy of the soldiers and the population, might lead his victorious army against Paris to reestablish the King's power."[20] Both Lafayette and Dumouriez would soon boost Marat's reputation for clairvoyance by attempting to fulfill that prophecy.

"It would be even better," Marat continued, if our soldiers "would wake up in time and finally drown all of their officers in their own blood!"[21] But with most of his readers now consumed by chauvinistic war fever, Marat was more out of step with public opinion than ever. Within days, however, Marat's grasp of the real dynamics of the Revolution was dramatically revealed when General Théobald Dillon was slain by mutinous troops who suspected him of treason. Marat hailed such acts as the highest expression of revolutionary patriotism.[22]

Marat's audacity enraged the Brissotin ministry. Fearful of the effect his seditious appeals might have on rank-and-file soldiers, the Legislative Assembly on May 3 ordered that Marat be arrested.[23] This was the first police action against Marat taken by the new "leftist" government, but it followed a familiar pattern. The printshop where *Ami du peuple* had most recently been printed was raided, but the People's Friend could not be apprehended because the authorities had no idea where to find him.

With police pursuit more intense than ever, Marat left the comforts of the Évrard sisters' home and went deeper into hiding. Publishing *Ami du peuple* also became more difficult, but he nevertheless was able to put out three or four issues a week throughout the month of May and the first half of June.

During the three weeks from June 15 though July 7, however, the journal did not appear at all.

Two politically significant events occurred in that critical three-week period. On June 20 a remarkable mobilization took place in Paris with all—or almost all—the characteristics of an insurrectionary action. A massive protest march of the people in arms was moving along in front of the royal palace when a side door was found to be unlocked. Whether that was accidental or whether the protestors had an accomplice inside the palace, demonstrators found their way to Louis XVI's private chambers. Lo and behold—there he was, completely unprotected. For many hours, thousands upon thousands of armed marchers filed past the monarch, all the while giving him an earful of their grievances. The procession continued until late in the evening, and while no physical harm befell the King, all he could do was sit and endure a considerable amount of verbal abuse. Wearing a revolutionary cap forced upon him by the demonstrators, he remained outwardly calm and wore a beneficent smile throughout the ordeal.

This was a stunning piece of revolutionary theater, but nothing came of it and Marat was completely unimpressed. The King had dismissed Roland and other Brissotins from the government on June 13, and the June 20 demonstration had been called to protest their removal. Marat saw it as a Brissotin affair from beginning to end—nothing more than a display of fake militancy.

Of far greater importance was an attempt a week later by Lafayette to militarily subdue the Revolution. He had left his army at the front and returned to Paris, where on June 28 he addressed the Legislative Assembly and demanded that the Jacobin Club be outlawed. Although the Assembly was not unsympathetic to Lafayette, when it vacillated he decided to take action on his own. He had not attempted to bring his troops to Paris with him (and it cannot be assumed that they would have followed him), so he attempted to mobilize the Parisian National Guard he had formerly commanded. He issued a call for the Guardsmen to march against the Jacobin Club and eradicate it as a center of political power, but few—at most a hundred—

responded. The fiasco earned him ridicule as a would-be Julius Caesar and he returned, humiliated, to the front.

Although Marat would not have wanted to see Lafayette's attempted putsch succeed, he was not at all happy with the way the affair ended. The National Guard and other patriots had merely *ignored* Lafayette, but if they had had any gumption, Marat believed, they would have risen against him and put an end to him once and for all. That Lafayette could attempt an overt military attack on the Revolution and then simply resume command of one of the armies charged with defense of the Revolution seemed to him beyond comprehension. The lack of a massive public response to this absurdity renewed the People's Friend's grave doubts about the people's seriousness, and several weeks later the July 22 *Ami du peuple* announced yet another retirement.

## FÉDÉRÉS TO THE RESCUE

The timing of this gloomy statement was peculiar because when it appeared it was completely at odds with Marat's behavior. He was clearly not withdrawing from the scene, but to the contrary was as active and energetic as ever. A week and a half earlier he had written a spirited appeal to the provincial National Guardsmen, the *fédérés*, who once again were converging on Paris for the annual July 14 celebration. He urged them to break open the arsenals and completely arm the people.[24]

Why, when he had been recharged with enthusiasm by the arrival of the *fédérés*, would he have issued such a despondent farewell on July 22? The most plausible answer is that his retirement announcement must have been sent to a printshop earlier, during the three-week period when he was unable to have anything printed, and then published on July 22 at the printer's initiative rather than Marat's.

Armed *fédérés* continued to stream into Paris from the provinces well after the Bastille Day celebration on July 14. The most famous contingent was a battalion from Marseilles, whose entrance into the capital on July 30 singing the *Marseillaise* gave the French Republic its national anthem. But the militiamen from Marseilles were to serve the Revolution in an even more important way by their crucial role in the great insurrection that would create the First Republic.

Marat had close connections with one of the key leaders of the Guardsmen from Marseilles, Charles Barbaroux. Before the Revolution Barbaroux had been a devoted follower of Marat's physics courses, and Marat had reestablished contact with him earlier that year. They would later become bitter political enemies, but in a letter of August 8, 1792, Barbaroux addressed Marat as "my dear teacher" and asked his forgiveness for not visiting him sooner.[25]

## THE "SECOND REVOLUTION" OF AUGUST 1792

Marat was in especially good spirits in early August. The tense military situation had deepened the radicalization. The people were awakening!

On July 30 a Coalition of Prussia and Austria had launched an invasion of France with the objective of occupying Paris. Two days later the infamous Brunswick Manifesto became known to the city's inhabitants. The commander of the Coalition army, the Duke of Brunswick, had threatened to destroy the city and massacre its inhabitants if any harm were to come to the King and his family. Far from intimidating Parisians, however, the Brunswick Manifesto had the opposite effect. It infuriated them and drove them into the arms of Marat, who for months had been loudly advocating that Louis XVI and his family be taken hostage and "held responsible for whatever happens."[26]

Marat was still in deep hiding, his movements concealed not only from the police but from historians of the Revolution. The details of his involvement in planning the great insurrection that erupted on August 10 are therefore unknown. It can be said, however, that the principal organizers were Cordeliers Club allies of the People's Friend such as Étienne Jean Panis, Étienne

François Garin, François Héron, and Antoine Joseph Santerre. Marat was meeting with them and with groups of *fédérés*, and his published calls to insurrection were at last getting the response he had always hoped for.

*Ami du peuple* did not appear during the last week of July and the first week of August, but it resurfaced on August 7 with another appeal "to the *Fédérés* of 83 Departments." On the night of August 9 the tocsin sounded the call to insurrection and the next morning the well-organized uprising was under way. The people of Paris, together with contingents of *fédérés*, assembled at the royal palace. The armed, well-disciplined crowd of about 20,000 easily overwhelmed the 1,200 or so troops defending the King, who sought refuge with the Legislative Assembly. The Assembly, however, having lost its moral authority among Parisians, was itself besieged and forced to submit to the command of a thoroughly reorganized Paris Commune. Louis XVI was relieved of his powers and imprisoned. The French monarchy ceased to exist.

The uprising of August 10 brought about the kind of social revolution that Marat had long been calling for. The new municipal government of Paris was formed by representatives of the 48 sections who were elected with no distinction between "active" and "passive" citizens. With the formerly passive citizens passive no longer, the Brissotins and other conservative politicians lost their artificial electoral advantage and political power passed to the radical Jacobin and Cordeliers leaders. The *sans-culottes* for the first time had begun to exercise political power.

The leaders of the insurrection held *de facto* power through their control of the Paris Commune, but to consolidate the new stage of the Revolution throughout France would require the formation of a legitimate national government. With that in mind, they called for elections to create a new governing body, the National Convention, to replace the Legislative Assembly. The elections were to be held on the basis of universal suffrage, which would make the Convention far more democratic than any of its predecessors. In fact, however, the suffrage was less than universal because the idea that women should have the right to vote was one whose time had not yet come.[27]

The new elections took time, so the first meeting of the Convention did not occur until September 20. Meanwhile, in the six weeks between August 10 and September 20 the Legislative Assembly, though largely discredited, continued to exist and to claim its legitimacy as the national government. A duality of power thus existed with the Legislative Assembly holding the official reins of government and the Paris Commune actually in command. The conflict played out in an interim six-member Council of Ministers that pitted Danton as Minister of Justice against Roland, the Brissotin leader who now held the post of Minister of the Interior.

## MARAT EMERGES FROM THE UNDERGROUND

Marat's circumstances were dramatically altered by the events of August 10. From that day forward he was no longer a hunted outlaw and was able to come out of hiding for good.[28] He had become a folk hero of sorts and could function openly as a political leader. He proclaimed his return to legality in a placard that appeared on the evening of August 10. It began dramatically: "A man who has been anathema for a long time escaped today from his underground hideout to try to consolidate the victory in your hands."[29]

The placard noted that the People's Friend's predictions about betrayals by the Legislative Assembly and the generals had all come true. It warned the people to not be complacent and proposed an action program to solidify their victory:

- Above all else, take the King and his wife and son hostage ... Make it plain to him that the Austrians and Prussians have two weeks to permanently retreat to a line twenty miles beyond the border or his head will roll.
- Seize all of the ex-ministers and lock them up.

- Execute all the counterrevolutionary members of the Parisian General Staff.
- Expel all the antipatriotic officers from their battalions.
- Disarm the infected battalions.
- Arm all patriotic citizens and generously supply them with ammunition.
- Demand the convocation of a National Convention to put the King on trial and to reform the constitution; above all, its members must not be chosen by an electoral assembly but by the direct vote of the people.[30]

Previously these proposals would have brought more charges of sedition down on Marat's head, but now he and the new Commune leaders were of like mind, as his proposal for a democratically elected Convention illustrates. Furthermore, with his allies now in power and his proposals more likely to be taken seriously, Marat's rhetoric had become considerably less violent and more "responsible." Rather than demanding that all enemies of the Revolution be put to death, he merely called for the former ministers and the counterrevolutionary officers to be imprisoned or dismissed from the army. The only exception was for traitors at the highest level of the military command, whose execution he continued to demand. That would include, above all, Lafayette.

Lafayette announced his intention to march on Paris but once again found his troops unwilling to follow, so on the night of August 19–20 he deserted his post and fled to Austria. Marat (who habitually called Lafayette by his family name) had long predicted that "the traitor Motier" would defect to the enemy, so Lafayette's departure gave fresh support once again to Marat's reputation as a prophet. Nonetheless, however gratified Marat may have felt to see his prediction come true, he was furious that Lafayette had been "allowed to escape."[31] The unfortunate general, however, did not find the reception he had hoped for in Austria. He was imprisoned and remained behind bars until 1796.

The new Paris Commune favored Marat and his fellow radical journalists by giving them printing presses that had been confiscated from the royal printshops. Marat received four presses, perhaps to make up for all the times in the past that the police had carted away his own presses. The decision was made by the Committee of Surveillance, the *de facto* executive committee of the Commune, a leadership body to which Marat himself was soon to be co-opted. He and Simonne Évrard moved into a new place at 30 Cordeliers Street and set up the presses there. Once again, Marat had become his own publisher.

*Ami du peuple* made its reappearance just three days after the insurrection, on August 13, but the journal had changed considerably in tone and content. Instead of denouncing the men in power, the People's Friend had joined their ranks. Rather than scolding the people for their lack of seriousness, he declared great confidence in them.

Now that he could finally avail himself of genuine freedom of the press, he felt less need to use it. In the following month only four issues of *Ami du peuple* and a few placards came off his presses. He hinted again that he might retire, but this time it was not out of discouragement but because his journal had accomplished its mission. Most of his attention was directed toward new responsibilities as a leader of the Commune, and toward preparations for the forthcoming elections to the Convention.

### THREATS OF WAR AND COUNTERREVOLUTION

Marat's retirement would have to wait, however; his newfound optimism proved to be premature. Far from being consolidated, the Revolution faced mounting threats from without and within. The enemies' armies had entered France and were steadily advancing toward Paris. At the same time, a major counterrevolutionary insurgency in the Vendée had begun to take shape.

On August 23 Longwy fell to the Prussians, removing the last obstacle blocking their march to the capital. By September 2 they had taken Verdun, less than 200 miles away. With Brunswick apparently about to make good on his threat to sack Paris, the city was in a state of panic.

The Commune called for volunteers to go to the front, and this time Marat was fully supportive. The war effort was no longer an irresponsible adventure; it was a defensive battle for survival. From Marat's point of view, the insurrection of August 10 had transformed France into a revolutionary nation worth defending. A placard he published on August 26 featured a theme that was a first for Marat: a call for social unity! He exhorted Parisians to "suspend for the moment all our hatreds, put aside all our dissension, and silence all our petty emotions in order to unite against our common enemy."[32] But two days later his earlier anxiety over traitors at home came to the fore again in a placard blasting the Legislative Assembly and the Brissotins.[33]

## THE SEPTEMBER MASSACRES

The vast majority of the Parisian population shared Marat's fear that counterrevolutionary elements in their midst could sabotage their defenses and leave the city helpless to stop Brunswick's troops from slaughtering them. On September 2 when news reached Paris that Verdun had fallen, panic gave rise to feverish action. Groups of several hundred armed *sans-culottes* converged upon jails where counterrevolutionaries were being held and over the next four days proceeded to kill more than a thousand inmates of nine prisons. A considerable number of the victims were not counterrevolutionaries, however, but simply petty criminals or people awaiting trial.

Although this vigilante action degenerated into an orgy of gratuitous violence, it had begun with a clear and rational purpose. The volunteers who were about to leave for the front lines were afraid that in their absence the counterrevolutionaries would escape from jail or be released by traitors. The women, children, and elderly who were left behind would be defenseless against them. This was not an unreasonable fear—it was a real danger that they thought had to be eliminated before they could march off to fight the Prussians.

At first, ad hoc tribunals attempted to distinguish between dangerous counterrevolutionaries and ordinary convicts, and about half the prisoners who were "tried" were spared. It was rough justice at best, and in the heat of the moment the process got out of hand. As the enemy armies drew nearer, impatience and frustration gained the upper hand and the executions became indiscriminate. The episode would become infamous as the September Massacres and would for good reason be condemned by future generations.

In the aftermath of the Revolution, during the period of the Thermidorian reaction, blame for organizing and directing the September Massacres began to be retrospectively attributed to Marat. No conscientious historian would give credence to that charge, but the myth of Marat's responsibility lives on in popular accounts of the French Revolution. The accusation is based on the fact that Marat had been a member of the Commune's leading council, the Committee of Surveillance, when the September Massacres took place. It was only on September 2, however, the day the prison executions began, that the Committee expanded from four to ten members, and Marat was among the six newcomers. Whatever the extent of his influence within the Committee may have been, he clearly did not have power of command over it.

Marat later defended the prison executions in principle and refused to condemn those who had carried them out, but he characterized them as "disastrous events" and expressed regret over the killing of petty criminals. The excesses, from his point of view, amounted to an unfortunate error rather than a crime.[34]

The insurrection of August 10 gave rise to a great leap forward in the revolutionary process, but the changes it brought about had only begun to unfold. Marat had moved to center stage, but bigger battles were yet to come.

# 5

# From the Convention Elections to the Assassination

## September 1792 to July 1793

In early September Marat's attention was not focused on the prison massacres, but on the elections to the Convention, scheduled to begin on September 3. He published four placards on the subject, two of which specified which candidates the People's Friend supported and which he opposed.[1]

Brissot and Condorcet headed the list of 35 candidates identified as "enemies of liberty," which also included a number of popular journalists and publishers such as Jean Louis Carra, Antoine Joseph Gorsas, Pierre Jean Audouin, Nicolas Bonneville, and Jean Baptiste Louvet. On the positive side of the ledger were the 22 candidates the People's Friend endorsed as "men deserving of the Nation's greatest esteem," among whom were Robespierre, Danton, Desmoulins, and Fréron.[2] The last of Marat's endorsements was for his alter ego:

> My friends, I'll finish by reminding you of the People's Friend. You know what he's done for the Nation; perhaps you don't know what he will continue to do for your happiness. The glory of being the foremost martyr of liberty is enough for him; if you overlook him—well, that's your misfortune.[3]

The election results demonstrated that Marat was in harmony with the Parisian electorate. None of those whom he opposed won election as the city's delegates to the Convention, although many of them were chosen to represent other parts of France. On the other side, 12 of those he supported, including himself, were among the 24 elected for Paris.

Marat found the procedures governing the Convention elections preferable to those of the past, but because they continued to include a two-stage system of balloting, he felt they were still not democratic enough. A first round of voting created electoral assemblies and then the electoral assemblies chose the Convention delegates. The latter process took several days to complete. The Parisian assembly's first choice, on September 5, was Robespierre, and the following day Danton was elected. By the fourth day Desmoulins and several more had joined the ranks of the winners.

Marat was not chosen until the fifth day. Although he was supported by a strong contingent of devoted followers, his reputation had also alienated a significant number of the assembly members. He might not have been elected at all had he not received Robespierre's endorsement. Robespierre did not mention Marat by name, but no one misunderstood his meaning when he urged them to vote for "the man who, in order to combat Lafayette and the court, had to keep himself hidden in cellars for a year."[4] On that same day, September 9, Marat was elected to the Convention with 420 out of 758 votes.[5]

Marat's election was a qualitative turning point in his political career. He did not cease his journalistic activities—in fact, his daily journal appeared more regularly than ever—but his effort and attention were from then on directed less toward the editor's desk and more toward the podium of the national parliament.

Marat was only one of 749 delegates to the Convention. He held no special title or position, and was at first deeply isolated from the vast majority of his fellow delegates. In spite of all that, he and his agenda soon became the central focus of the Convention's concerns. He did not dominate it in the sense of being able to dictate its policies, but he did dominate its consciousness. A few months later a hostile delegate groused: "Do you remember our first sessions? Hardly a member would even sit next to him. Now he gets the floor endlessly."[6]

## MARAT GOES TO THE MOUNTAIN

A dramatic change in Marat's political approach and public persona accompanied his rise to the national political stage.

Previously he had been agitating for the overthrow of a reactionary government. Now he was putting all his effort toward upholding a revolutionary regime.

Marat did not try to disguise the transformation. To the contrary, he wanted it known far and wide that he had embarked on a *nouvelle marche*—a "new course." To emphasize it he changed the name of his journal from *Ami du peuple* to *Journal de la République Française* (*JRF*). The final issue of *Ami du peuple* appeared on September 21, 1792, and the first with the new masthead came off the presses four days later.

In layout and design *JRF* appeared virtually identical to its predecessor, as if the name were the only thing that was new about it. Its political content, however, had undergone a sharp change of direction. Whereas the final issue of *Ami du peuple* had attacked the new Convention and called upon the people to rise up and overthrow it (even though he was in it), the first issue of *JRF* recognized the legitimacy of *part* of the Convention and declared that the People's Friend would subordinate himself to its leadership. "I am ready to follow the road that the defenders of the people believe most effective," he wrote, "I must march alongside them."[7]

The part of the Convention that Marat vowed to follow was its left wing, known as the Mountain because its members sat in banks of seats elevated above those of the other delegates. The 24 Parisian deputies constituted the Mountain's central core, but they had the solid support of 50 or 60 other members. When the Convention first met, the *Montagnards*—men of the Mountain—represented only about 10 percent of its voting strength.

At the other end of the political spectrum, the Convention's right wing was made up of politicians who had previously adhered to Brissot's faction. Brissot was still among them, but his leadership had been eclipsed by others, so the term "Brissotin" had become outdated. Marat called them "Roland's faction" or, sarcastically, "the statesmen." Historians retrospectively dubbed them the *Girondins*. The Girondins were not a sharply defined group of delegates, but they nonetheless constituted a relatively

stable right wing with approximately twice the voting strength
of the Montagnards.

The left- and right-wing groupings together comprised less
than 30 percent of the Convention's delegates, which meant that
more than 70 percent constituted a centrist majority crucial to
the outcome of any particular vote. With no political principles
or policies of their own, the centrists—known as "the Plain" (or
less charitably, "the Swamp")—could not lead the Convention,
but could only throw their weight behind initiatives proposed
by the Montagnards or the Girondins. The Convention thus
became a political battlefield in a war over the votes of the Plain.

Marat vowed to "march alongside" the Mountain, but
that is not to say that he *was* a Montagnard. He considered
himself independent of them—an outsider willing to collaborate
with them, but an outsider nonetheless. He didn't rule out the
possibility, however, that he might at some future time actually
join the Mountain. Marat believed that unity among the
revolutionary forces was the foremost necessity of the moment,
and to accomplish it would require him to advocate polices of
moderation that did not come naturally for him. Not one to do
anything halfway, however, once he made his decision he carried
it through to the end.

Collaboration with the Mountain meant that Marat would
have to become an active participant at the Jacobin Club,
where the Montagnards hashed out their strategy and tactics
before doing battle on the floor of the Convention. After the
tumultuous events of August 10, membership in the Jacobin
Club became more accessible to less affluent patriots. Then in
October Brissot and his allies were forced out. On the very day
of Brissot's expulsion Marat made his first appearance there,[8]
and within a few months had become one of the Jacobins' most
prominent leaders.

The coming together of Marat and the Mountain can be better
understood as a merger between two political currents rather
than as an individual joining a political organization. Prior to
the insurrection of August 10 Marat had always functioned as
a solo act in the political field. Although he was a freelancer

with no political party at his command, he nonetheless had a significant following that was quite distinct from the segment of the population that looked to the Mountain for leadership.

The social composition of the Jacobins hardly differed at all from that of the Girondins. Robespierre and his cothinkers were radical democrats who sympathized with the *sans-culottes*, but they were not the political representatives of the urban poor. Marat, by contrast, had won the admiration and trust of the *sans-culottes* after three years of championing their cause as the intrepid People's Friend. He now believed that the urban poor and the radical democrats needed to combine their strength in order to consolidate and advance the Revolution. A few months earlier he had provided the theoretical basis for that conclusion by appealing to historical experience:

> Pushed to despair by excesses of tyranny, peoples have tried a hundred times to break their chains.
>
> They are always successful when an entire nation revolts against despotism. Such a case is extremely rare; it is much more common to see a nation split into two parties, one *for* and the other *against* the despot.
>
> When each of these parties is made up of a variety of social classes, the one that is against the despotism succeeds rather easily in crushing it, because in that case there are more advantages for the attackers in overthrowing it than there are for the defenders in maintaining it. Such was the case with the Swiss, the Dutch, the English, and the Americans.
>
> But that never happens when the plebeians—that is, the lower classes of the nation—are alone in the struggle against the upper classes. [9]

Marat's "new course" aimed at avoiding the social isolation of the *sans-culottes* that would inevitably lead to their defeat. It was designed to create and solidify an alliance uniting the urban poor with the radical democrats of the Jacobin Club. Marat's unique place in the history of the French Revolution arose from his ability to play a leadership role in those two distinct but critically important political arenas, and to bring them together.

The more timid among the Jacobins were hesitant at first to look favorably upon Marat's overtures. Fearful of his reputation as a wild-eyed firebrand, they felt that association with him would alienate the Plain and make it impossible for the Mountain to win crucial votes in the Convention. In December a motion for Marat's expulsion from the Jacobin Club, although ultimately rejected, was greeted with both cheers and jeers from the membership.[10] But during the early months of 1793 it became increasingly evident to the Jacobin leaders that their struggle to preserve the fragile new Republic could not succeed without the ardent support of the *sans-culottes*. Marat's value in their eyes rose in proportion with their desire to strengthen their alliance with the urban poor.

## MARAT ADDRESSES THE CONVENTION

The inaugural session of the Convention was held on September 20, 1792. Two days later it proclaimed the existence of the first French Republic and the official abolition of the monarchy.

Marat's arrival at the Convention caused a sensation. Most of the delegates, especially those from the provinces, had only heard of him, and what they had heard was not favorable. Some expected to see a monster; others were surprised to find out that the People's Friend was not a fictional character, like Hébert's Père Duchesne. Now the fire-breathing apostle of revolutionary violence was among them, in the flesh—an elected representative of the Nation with status equal to their own.

Marat, like most of the regular deputies, lay low and said nothing during the first few sessions. On September 25, however, the Girondins forced him into the spotlight by launching an attack against him. The idea was to make a bogeyman of Marat as a way to frighten the Plain into their own arms. Marat, they asserted, was a stalking horse for Danton's and Robespierre's plans to create a revolutionary dictatorship. Trying to demonize Marat, however, was a strategy that would end in disaster for the Gironde.

Danton tried to appease the Girondins by virtually disowning Marat. Robespierre was not as conciliatory as

Marat, pistol in hand, addresses the Convention for the first time.
("Jean Paul Marat Inciting Revolution," drawn by Eugene Joseph Viollat,
engraved by Stephane Pannemaker)

Danton, but he also failed to come to Marat's defense. It was
left to Marat to stand up for himself, setting the stage for one
of the most dramatic parliamentary debuts of any time or
country. When the People's Friend approached the podium, he
was greeted by a boisterous chant orchestrated by the Girondins:
"*Sit down! Sit down!*" He had been given the floor, however,
so he simply waited for the commotion to subside. At the first

opportunity, he declared: "I have a great number of personal enemies in this assembly."[11]

"*All of us! All of us!*" came the reply.

"Have you no shame?" Marat said above the din. "Listen to me for a moment and I won't abuse your patience." The assembly quieted and Marat was able to continue. Danton and Robespierre should not be blamed for advocating a revolutionary dictatorship, he told them; they *rejected* the idea. That was unfortunate, he added, because he continued to believe it was necessary.[12]

Apparently surprised that the man addressing them did not fit the description of the dreadful fiend they had been led to expect, the assembly heard Marat out. The Girondins attempted to regain the momentum by calling Marat an outlaw and pointing out that there were still outstanding warrants for his arrest. Some of the Mountain delegates countered that the arrest warrants had been issued by former officials who had since been thoroughly discredited—above all, Lafayette.

But the Girondins believed they held a trump card. One of them held up a copy of the final issue of *Ami du peuple* and read from it Marat's call for a new insurrection to overthrow the Convention. Having swung the majority of the delegates back to their side, the Girondins made a motion to arrest Marat on the spot and charge him with sedition. Two bailiffs took up positions alongside Marat, ready to arrest him if the motion passed.

This was a pivotal moment. If the vote had gone against him and he had been tried and found guilty of sedition, he could have been executed. He demanded the right to speak in his own defense, and was again given the floor. He began by expressing pride in the arrest decrees previously brought against him by the traitors of the National Assembly and the Legislative Assembly. All of those indictments, he declared, had been rendered null and void by the people when they elected him to the Convention.

As for the call for a new insurrection that had appeared in his journal a week earlier, yes, he had written it; and yes, he had meant every word of it. But in the meantime it had become outdated, and it no longer represented his point of view. To prove it, he pulled out a copy of the first issue of his new periodical, the *JRF*, which had appeared that very day, and read the editorial proclaiming his new course. This was designed to assure the Plain that he posed no threat to them, and to show the Mountain that he was intent on not embarrassing them.[13]

The tension in the assembly hall diminished and the moment of danger for Marat passed. Although it is unlikely that one speech won him the trust of the majority, it sufficed to demonstrate that he was not the phantasmagorical monster the Girondins had made him out to be. What saved Marat was that the Plain no longer feared him enough to establish the precedent of indicting an elected member of the Convention.

Before returning to his seat, the ever-dramatic People's Friend could not resist indulging in a bit of political theater. Pulling a pistol from his waistband and putting it to his head, he exclaimed: "If you had passed an arrest decree against me, this gun would have removed me from the rage of my persecutors—I would have blown my brains out at this very podium!"[14] A man with a reputation for wildness wielding a pistol in a crowded assembly hall might seem to be a recipe for chaos, but the delegates did not panic. The handguns of that era were not terribly threatening. Marat's firearm was capable of but a single inaccurate shot without reloading, but it would have been good enough to take his own life. The main result of the spectacle was that Marat had once again stolen the spotlight and focused it on himself.

The apparently inconsistent way the Convention delegates treated Marat calls for explanation. Why would they shout him down at one moment and listen quietly the next? For one thing, a great deal of the response was organized by the Girondins, and although they would generally be howling at him, there were times when they wanted him to be heard, hoping he would make some outlandish statement that would discredit himself and the Mountain. More important, however, was Marat's ability to *command* the respect of an initially hostile audience by remaining perfectly calm at the center of a maelstrom and projecting an air of supreme self-confidence. Almost every commentator marveled at Marat's *sang-froid*—a preternatural coolness under fire.

Another crucial reason for Marat's success at the podium arose from the fact that the Convention delegates were not deliberating in a vacuum. The assembly hall included public galleries filled with Parisian *sans-culottes* supportive of the People's Friend. Although the observers could not officially participate in the proceedings, their vociferous expressions of agreement or displeasure often made a profound impression on the vacillating delegates of the Plain.

The divisions between the left and right wings of the Convention were geographically based. The Mountain's delegates were mostly representatives of Parisian districts, where the Jacobin Club had controlled the electoral assemblies. The Girondins had likewise dominated the electoral machinery in certain other parts of France, and the delegates of the Plain also hailed from the provinces. The Girondins therefore sought to turn the political struggle between left and right into a territorial war between Paris and the provinces.

Portraying themselves as defenders of the whole nation's interests against the selfish desires of Parisian radicals, the Girondins called upon the provinces to resist the extension of centralized power emanating from the capital city. In response, the Mountain denounced the Girondins as "federalists" who were trying to destroy the unity of the one and indivisible Nation. A Girondin motion to move the Convention out of the capital (and therefore out of reach of the *sans-culottes'* intimidation) was condemned by the Mountain as a conspiracy to organize the provinces for a military strike against Paris.

The Girondins saw Marat as a splendid symbol of Parisian radicalism that could be used to reinforce provincial prejudices against the "rabble" of France's great metropolis. By incessantly citing his earlier writings, they depicted Marat as the evangel of anarchy, sedition, and civil war, and tarred the Mountain with guilt by association.

The People's Friend, however, was an experienced polemicist and fully capable of returning their fire. In his journal as well as on the Convention floor he blasted them as traitors and villains. His approach, however, was not simply one-dimensional all-out attack. In accord with his new course, he advised the impatient *sans-culottes* to remain calm and *not* rise up immediately to wipe out the Girondins. Those who failed to heed his counsel and continued to agitate for a new insurrection found themselves denounced by the People's Friend as *agents provocateurs.*

He cautioned his readers against provocations that the Girondins could turn to their advantage to mobilize the provinces against Paris. "Parisians will prevent that disaster by their moderation," he wrote.

> It's the people's friend—always depicted by the traitors as a fire-breathing extremist—who is asking you to be moderate in the name of the public well-being. Just a few more days and the infernal clique will be completely unmasked; so the Convention will open its eyes, and only then will it be able to work to save the Republic.[15]

Marat obviously believed a showdown with the right-wing faction was imminent and inevitable.


## THE DUMOURIEZ AFFAIR

The "traitors" Marat tirelessly condemned included not only the Girondin politicians, but also the aristocratic military leaders, with Dumouriez at the head of the list. On November 29 an astonishing prophecy appeared in *JRF* that proved to be one of his most accurate. "A hundred to one," he wagered, "that Dumouriez will defect before the end of next March."[16]

Dumouriez in fact did not go over to the Austrians until April 2, 1793, so Marat would have lost that bet. Missing the exact date by only two days, however, confirmed the acuity of Marat's political insight. At the time Marat made his prophecy, no one else would have imagined that Dumouriez could do what Lafayette had done. On the very day that the Convention opened, September 20, Dumouriez defeated the Prussians at Valmy, raising his prestige among the revolutionary public to new heights. Marat's prediction that the "hero of Valmy" would soon betray the Revolution was audacious, to say the least.

Marat's prophecy, however, was not a lucky guess. His distrust of Dumouriez had been aroused by an incident that had come to his attention at the beginning of October. Further information that dissident soldiers subsequently supplied to the People's Friend confirmed his suspicions. The incident involved the execution of four men by soldiers under Dumouriez's command. Dumouriez condemned the executions as unjustified and punished the two battalions he held responsible for them. In the Convention, the Girondins echoed Dumouriez's claim that the four men had been Prussian deserters who should not have been mistreated, much less executed, after surrendering peacefully to French forces.

Marat, on the other hand, suspected that rank-and-file Parisian volunteers were being falsely accused as part of the effort to discredit revolutionary Paris. The nub of the issue was the identity of the four men who had been executed. Had they really been Prussian deserters, as Dumouriez said, or were they, as Marat's sources told him, French émigrés who had been caught in the act of espionage? If they were counterrevolutionary spies, Marat said, the Parisian battalions who executed them deserved praise, not punishment.

Marat's journal of course expressed strong support for the soldiers, but now he was in a position to do more than editorialize. As a Convention delegate, he could make a parliamentary issue of it. In another manifestation of his new course, rather than acting in an individual capacity he sought the support of the Jacobin Club before taking the fight to the floor of the Convention. His first visit to the Jacobins was on October 12.[17] Two days later, Dumouriez himself appeared at the Jacobin Club, receiving a rousing ovation and high praise from Danton.[18] Then the following day, October 15, Marat asked that they conduct an investigation into the "Prussian deserters" incident, and his request was granted. The Jacobins appointed a three-member commission of inquiry, which included Marat.[19]

## CRASHING DUMOURIEZ'S PARTY

A gala social event honoring Dumouriez was held on October 16 at the home of a famous actor named François-Joseph Talma. It was supposed to be simply an opportunity for Parisian high society to rub elbows with the hero of Valmy, but the People's Friend had other ideas. He thought it would be a perfect time to ask Dumouriez a few questions, so he led his commission of inquiry to Talma's house with the party in full swing.

Talma's guests watched in astonishment as Marat and his two co-inquisitors marched up to the guest of honor and pressed an unwelcome interview upon him. Although Talma must have resented the intrusion, he could not have helped but appreciate the theatricality of the moment. The costumes alone were enough to lay bare the class nature of the political confrontation: Marat in the scruffy plebeian garb of the *sans-culottes* surrounded by Girondins, all aghast in their finest formal attire.

The testy interview ended with Dumouriez turning his back on the three Jacobins.[20] As soon as Marat and his colleagues had departed, one of Talma's fellow actors, Dugazon, ostentatiously squirted perfume throughout the hall in a doubly symbolic gesture. In addition to purifying the air that Marat's revolutionary politics had polluted, it protected the sensitive nostrils of the beautiful people from the unpleasant aromas of the lower classes.

Although the interview itself produced nothing of value, the disdain with which the general treated the commission of inquiry convinced Marat more than ever of his treasonous intentions. The following day Marat asked for and received an order from the Convention's Committee of Surveillance allowing his commission access to Ministry of War documents concerning the disputed incident at the front. At the Convention on October 18, Marat demanded Dumouriez's arrest.[21] He could not have had a realistic expectation of his motion's passing; among the delegates he was almost totally isolated, and especially on this issue. Over the following two months, however, he was able to arrange the Parisian soldiers' release from prison and to win official rehabilitation for their two battalions.

All the while, the Girondins continued to rail against Marat on the floor of the Convention, and still the Mountain made no effort to defend him. His former friend and pupil Barbaroux bitterly assailed him in a placard that was signed by all of the delegates from Marseilles. Many of the *fédérés* from that city who revered the People's Friend were perplexed by Barbaroux's attack. When Marat met with some of them in an effort to give them his side of the story, Barbaroux rose in the Convention to charge Marat with trying to foment civil war. Once again, a chorus of calls for Marat's arrest filled the assembly hall.

Marat tried to respond but was unable to make himself heard above the din. He simply stood at the podium, waiting, until eventually the uproar subsided. Although almost every phrase he uttered elicited angry shouts from his audience, he continued nonetheless: "You're always talking about factions. Sure, there's a faction here; it's the one that's lined up against me! As for me, I stand alone, since not a single one among you [he turned to face the Mountain] has the courage to speak in my defense."[22] Once again Marat's *sang-froid* prevailed. The delegates settled down and he was able to proceed. After he ridiculed Barbaroux's accusations, the Convention effectively disposed of them by assigning them to a committee for "further study." The Girondins were infuriated at having been foiled again.

Barbaroux escalated his attack by organizing right-wing soldiers to march in the streets against Marat and burn him in effigy. Marat was incredulous: "Who would believe that only three months ago" this man was proclaiming eternal friendship?[23] On the last day of October Barbaroux's thugs gathered around Marat's residence and threatened to burn it down, prompting Marat to go back into hiding for the first time since he had emerged from the underground. On November 3 a demonstration of several hundred soldiers went further by demanding not only Marat's head but Robespierre's and Danton's as well.

This new display of military backing encouraged the Girondins to continue their efforts to have Marat arrested. In hiding and prevented from attending the Convention, Marat called on the

Jacobins and the Mountain to stand up for him. Their response was slow to materialize. Danton again attempted to appease the Girondins by acknowledging that Marat was an offensive character and promising that he would not escape justice if found guilty of any crimes. Robespierre, however, was more farsighted and courageous than Danton. He knew that the ultimate target of the right-wing faction was not Marat but the Mountain, and himself in particular. Defending Marat had thus become a matter of self-preservation for Robespierre, so he rallied the Mountain to combat the anti-Marat campaign.

Robespierre could not silence Marat's enemies, but he at least created enough space for the People's Friend to resume an above-ground existence. His journal reappeared after having been shut down for five days. Although Marat continued to complain, and justifiably so, that the Mountain's efforts to protect him had been insufficient, that was beginning to change. As the Mountain began to accept him not only as a legitimate member of the Convention but as a spokesman for their faction, his virtual isolation within the legislative body came to an end.

## THE TRIAL AND EXECUTION OF LOUIS XVI

Another reason that the campaign against Marat eased up was that the Girondins found themselves on the defensive with regard to the most pressing political problem of the moment: whether or not the deposed monarch, Louis XVI—thenceforth simply "Louis Capet"—should be executed as a traitor. The Girondins were nominally republicans, but they had become dependent upon the support of royalists and constitutional monarchists who saw them as a "lesser evil" than the Jacobins, and who expected them to save the former King's life. On the other hand, the Girondins couldn't openly defend his innocence without making *themselves* vulnerable to a charge of treason.

Marat compounded the Girondins' problems by proposing, and winning, a very significant procedural ruling. He took the floor of the Convention on December 6 and demanded, "Let the death of the tyrant be voted upon by voice roll-call vote, and let the vote be taken publicly."[24] The vote for or against executing Louis Capet would then become a litmus test of devotion to the Revolution, and eliminating the secret ballot meant that delegates could not hide their vote. All four of the crucial votes were taken according to Marat's motion.

First, on January 15, 1793, came the vote on Louis's guilt or innocence. There was no room for doubt that he was guilty, because on November 20 a cache of letters proving his collusion with the Revolution's mortal enemies had been discovered hidden in the palace walls. All but 26 of the 719 delegates present voted "Guilty."

But should the guilty traitor be executed or not? The Girondins made a motion for a national referendum on the question—an "appeal to the people"—that would relieve the Convention of responsibility for making the fateful decision. It was presented as an exercise in direct democracy, but many delegates saw the wisdom in Marat's depiction of the motion as a perfect formula for igniting a civil war. It was defeated 424 to 283.

The following day, January 16, the third vote—the historic one on the death penalty—was taken. It was a time-consuming process because delegates were allowed to make statements for the record to explain their votes. Marat cast his with these words:

> In the firm conviction that Louis was the principal author of the crimes that led to so much bloodshed on August 10, and of all the massacres that have soiled France during the Revolution, I vote that the tyrant be put to death within twenty-four hours.[25]

When they were tallied, there were 361 votes definitely in favor of the death penalty, 334 definitely against, and 26 that were ambiguous. Even if the unclear votes had been added to the "nays," the decision to execute the former monarch would have passed by a single vote.

A fourth vote, on January 18, resulted from a final desperate attempt by the Girondins to reverse the momentous decision. A motion to postpone the execution was voted down 380 to 310.

On January 21, 1793, the issue was settled when a guillotine blade ended the life of Louis Capet, formerly Louis XVI. Two days later Marat wrote: "The tyrant's head has just fallen beneath the sword of the law. That blow has overturned the foundations of the monarchy among us. Now I finally believe in the Republic!"[26]

Marat's assessment was correct. Guillotining the King was powerful testimony to the irreversibility of the Revolution. It was a slap-in-the-face challenge to the crowned heads of Europe as well as to the royalist forces within France. In the months following the execution, the military coalition arrayed against the Revolution would be joined by England, Spain, and Holland, and a counterrevolutionary revolt would break out in the Vendée in western France. The Revolution found itself besieged on all sides. When Louis was put to death, all hope of peaceful compromise died with him.

The day after the execution, a deputy who had voted for the death penalty was assassinated in a café. Although the assassin, a royalist, was apprehended, swiftly tried, and guillotined, his deed had significant political consequences. To defend itself, the Mountain felt compelled to deepen its ties with Marat and the social forces he spoke for. The alliance between the People's Friend and the Mountain was a thoroughgoing merger that transformed both partners. Marat thus emerged as a legitimate political leader, both at the Jacobin Club and at the Convention.

## A CHALLENGE FROM THE LEFT

While the King's trial was dominating the consciousness of the political class, the rapidly rising price of bread was creating hunger and turmoil among the poorer classes. The most radicalized of the Parisian *sans-culottes* began to be attracted to a new group of militant agitators such as Jacques Roux, Jean Varlet, and Théophile Leclerc. They were called *Enragés*, which literally meant "madmen," but they accepted the name with pride. The *Enragés* stood for direct democracy and called on the government to enforce price maximums on necessary commodities, starting with bread. Because rampaging inflation of the paper money, the *assignat*, was driving the poor ever deeper into misery, the *Enragés* demanded that the government bring the *assignat* under control by enforcing the stability of its value.

The *Enragés* venerated the People's Friend and believed they were following in his footsteps. Jacques Roux, who in December had become a member of the municipal government, called himself "the Marat of the Commune." Marat, however, did not return their admiration. On February 12 the *Enragés* led a delegation representing Paris's 48 sections to the bar of the Convention to demand that speculators in wheat be punished. They undoubtedly assumed Marat would support them, but he did not. They aimed their fiery oratory against the Convention as a whole, including the Mountain, and Marat now considered himself a Montagnard.

Marat advised the *Enragé* spokesmen to calm down, but when they refused to tone down their confrontational assault he responded in kind. He characterized their demands as "excessive, bizarre, and subversive of all good order," and demanded that "those who have wasted the Convention's time in this manner be prosecuted for disturbing the peace."[27] No one had expected that. The People's Friend was calling on the police to suppress ultraradicals! As an indication of how topsy-turvy this must have appeared to those unaware of Marat's "new course," the Girondin leader Buzot commended Marat's contribution to the debate.[28] The *Enragé* delegation won almost no support from the Convention.

What was the meaning of this astonishing turnabout? Had Marat forsaken his principles and "sold out"? On the surface it would seem that what Marat was now saying was sharply opposed to his previous stance. In fact, many of the *Enragés'* statements that he condemned as counterrevolutionary were verbatim quotations from his own writings. But Marat was not being erratic or hypocritical. There had been a fundamental change in the political context, and he had altered his tactics to take the new situation into account. The essential goal remained unchanged: completion of the social revolution.

When the *Enragés* quoted Marat's 1792 denunciations of the Legislative Assembly and claimed that the same applied to the Convention, Marat adamantly disagreed. In his eyes the Legislative Assembly had been completely hopeless, but the Convention was not, despite its weaknesses due to the Girondin element. The Girondins, he believed, could be disposed of and then the Convention would be a powerful instrument of social revolution.

Marat feared that the ultraleftist agitation of the *Enragés* would mislead or confuse the *sans-culottes* and thereby sabotage his attempt to ally them with the Mountain. Moreover, both Marat and the Mountain were aware that ultraradical actions in Paris would isolate the capital from the rest of France and give the counterrevolution an easy victory. Marat had not begun to preach moderation because he had suddenly become conservative, but because he believed the *Enragés*' ultraleft antics posed a grave danger to the Revolution.[29]

The People's Friend had earlier responded to a reader who asked how long his new policy of moderation would last by saying, "Until the tyrant is gone and the Roland faction is defeated."[30] The first of those two tasks had been accomplished, but the second remained. Time, Marat believed, favored the Mountain. The Girondins were on the verge of being exposed as the counterrevolutionaries they really were, and then all good patriots throughout France—not just Parisian radicals alone—would drive them from power.

Marat knew full well, however, that the grievances expressed by the *Enragés* at the Convention were genuine. Food shortages and skyrocketing food prices were driving poor Parisians below the subsistence level. The analysis and conclusions Marat put forth in the February 25 issue of his journal were as radical as anything the *Enragés* had said:

> It is undeniable that the capitalists, the speculators, the monopolists, the luxury merchants, etc., etc., are all, to one degree or another, supporters of the old regime who miss their old profitable scams by which they

enriched themselves at the public's expense. How could they, then, concur in good faith with the establishment of the reign of freedom and equality? Given the impossibility of changing their hearts, and having no hope of seeing the legislature take strong measures to force such a change, I see the total destruction of that accursed race as the only way to establish tranquility in the State.

Today they redouble their zeal to reduce the people to misery by the exorbitant rise in the price of staple foods and the fear of famine. The Nation, fed up with these disgusting troubles, will itself take on the responsibility of purging the earth of that criminal race, which cowardly elected officials encourage to crime with impunity. No one should find it odd that the people, pushed to despair, impose their own justice. In all countries where the rights of the people are more than empty words ... the looting of a few stores, at the door of which the monopolists are hanged, soon puts an end to the embezzlement that reduces millions of people to despair and has caused millions to perish in poverty.[31]

On the day this article was published—but before it actually appeared on the streets—a semi-spontaneous "fair price" movement began to spread through Paris. Organized groups of *sans-culottes* invaded grocery stores and rather than simply looting the goods they found there, they set prices they considered fair for sugar, soap, and other necessary commodities, and paid for them. The shop owners, needless to say, considered this to be simply another form of looting. Marat's article could not have initiated this movement, but it may well have encouraged its continuance.

Marat had not *advocated* lynching and looting—he had *predicted* those consequences if the government failed to act. His article had in fact proposed a specific way to render lynchings unnecessary through the creation of a revolutionary tribunal with the power to prosecute criminal speculators. But if the government failed in its duty to protect the people, then the people would have no choice but to act in self-defense.

Although it was a case of blaming the messenger for bad news, the Girondins nevertheless accused Marat of provoking the food riots and again demanded his arrest. Marat in turn attacked the Girondins by charging that the riots had been fomented by their agents as part of their plot to turn the provinces against Paris. The Mountain came to Marat's defense this time and the attack was repelled.

Meanwhile, in early March the Coalition's armies invaded Belgium, and when the news reached Paris that General Dumouriez had left Belgium unprotected, it almost triggered another insurrection. By March 10 the city was inundated with protests calling for his arrest and for the removal of the Girondins from the Convention. Given Marat's longstanding denunciations of Dumouriez and the Girondins, his response was again not what might have been expected. He was strongly opposed to an insurrectionary movement forcing these demands upon the Convention at that moment. Timing was of the utmost importance.

Robespierre and Marat both knew that they could easily mobilize the Parisian *sans-culottes* to march upon the Convention and impose their will upon it, but that would appear to the provinces as a naked power grab. The Girondins could then unite the rest of France to defeat an isolated Paris and reverse the course of the Revolution. If they were patient, however, the military crisis would soon make it obvious to the public opinion of the provinces that Dumouriez and the Girondins were in cahoots with France's enemies and should be eliminated.

A delegation heavily influenced by the *Enragés* went to the Convention on March 12 and demanded that Dumouriez be arrested immediately. Marat's polemics against that proposal seemed especially paradoxical, as he appeared to be defending Dumouriez. An attack on Dumouriez at this moment, Marat said, was an attack on the military defenses of the Revolution.[32] The *Enragé* delegation was therefore abetting a counterrevolutionary conspiracy. The Girondins again unexpectedly found themselves applauding Marat.[33]

## THE DENOUEMENT OF THE DUMOURIEZ AFFAIR

The following week, however, Dumouriez's communiqués to the Convention took on an obviously threatening tone, prompting Marat to return to an all-out offensive against him. Unnerved by

the general's aggressiveness, the Convention leaders appointed
Danton to lead a commission to the front to assess his intentions.
This kowtowing was unacceptable to Marat, who published
a harsh diatribe against Dumouriez in the March 20 issue of
his journal.[34]

The following day, March 21, Parisians learned of Dumouriez's
critical defeat at Neerwinden and the recapture of Brussels by the
Austrians. Dumouriez had the bad grace to blame the fiasco on
his soldiers. Marat immediately went on the attack against the
general, but the rest of the Mountain vacillated. Danton, who
had previously favored a conciliatory approach, had returned
from his meeting with Dumouriez and seemed hesitant to share
his findings with the Convention. Marat at first appeared totally
isolated, but Robespierre and his faction soon enlisted in his
campaign against Dumouriez. Marat was no longer following
the Mountain; the Mountain was following Marat.

The reports of the military debacle in Belgium were
accompanied by more bad news. A major counterrevolutionary
uprising had erupted in western France, in the Vendée region.
The simultaneous internal and external threats to the Revolution
apparently led Marat to decide that a new insurrection in Paris
was now on the agenda. On March 27 he sounded the warning
at the Jacobin Club: "I ask that all the sections of Paris assemble
to challenge the Convention: Does it have the means to save the
Nation? If it doesn't, then the people must declare that they are
ready to save the Nation themselves."[35]

Marat was still perturbed, however, by the continuing
indecisiveness of the Mountain, whose leadership he believed was
of crucial importance. He was especially annoyed at Danton's
procrastination with regard to his report on Dumouriez. He did
not think Danton was conspiring with Dumouriez, but felt he
had deluded himself into thinking that conciliation was possible.
On March 29 Marat demanded that Danton stop stalling and
give his report.[36]

Finally, on March 30, Danton presented his account of the
meeting with Dumouriez, but it was vague and uninformative.[37]
On March 31, at the Jacobin Club, Marat challenged Danton

to "swear with me an oath to die to save the Nation!"[38] After Danton complied, Marat received a virtually unanimous ovation from the Jacobins' membership when he called upon them to arm the people and organize them for action.

By this time Dumouriez had openly threatened to lead his army to Paris to rid the Convention of Marat, Robespierre, and their supporters.[39] That gave the Mountain all the motive it needed to stiffen its backbone and take action against Dumouriez and his Girondin allies. The Jacobins were ready to fight, but on April 1 Marat told them: "We'll have to strike great blows, but the moment hasn't arrived yet; I'll let you know when it's time."[40] Marat sensed that the threat to march on Paris was a bluff. When Dumouriez, like Lafayette before him, found that his troops would not follow him on a counterrevolutionary mission, he too defected to the Austrians. When the shocking news of his betrayal reached Paris on April 3, Marat's reputation as a prophet reached its apogee.

Marat's newfound influence was further confirmed by the advent of two institutions that he had long campaigned for: the Revolutionary Tribunal and the Committee of Public Safety. On March 9 the Convention established the Revolutionary Tribunal, a special court to try cases involving counterrevolutionary activity. Then, on April 5, the creation of the Committee of Public Safety fulfilled Marat's incessant demand for a special commission with extraordinary powers to investigate and prosecute treasonous conspiracies. Both were prompted by Parisians' mounting fears over the military crisis. The Committee of Public Safety would later become the center of power in the Jacobin Republic.

## PRESIDENCY OF THE JACOBIN CLUB

In early April Marat was elected president of the Jacobin Club for the first and only time. The office was largely symbolic and its term was only ten sessions, but what it symbolized was the rise of Marat's credibility in the eyes of the Jacobin membership and the definitive end of his political isolation.

It so happened that he presided over only a single meeting of the Jacobins, on April 5, and his participation lasted only a few minutes. It was not an important session, but it turned out to have significant consequences for Marat. He arrived late, thanked the members for honoring him with the presidency, recognized a speaker, signed a paper, and left early to attend a committee meeting at the Convention.[41] Marat did not read the paper he had been handed to sign; he simply affixed his signature in his capacity as president. It was a declaration, formulated by one of the Club's committees, to be sent out to Jacobin organizations in the provinces. It read in part: "Brothers and friends, your greatest dangers are in your midst ... Yes, the counterrevolution is in the government, in the National Convention. That's where it has to be smashed! Arise, republicans![42]

In the political context of that moment it was not a particularly radical manifesto. It demanded that the Girondins be expelled from the Convention, but did not go as far as the *Enragés*, who called for their arrest and execution. Its call for patriots in the provinces to arm themselves and come to Paris, however, was sufficiently provocative to serve as a new pretext for an attack on Marat at the Convention.

### MARAT ON TRIAL

Dumouriez's defection angered revolutionary Paris, but the removal of his threat to sack the city led to a momentary decrease in political tension. That and the fact that a significant percentage of the Montagnard delegates were off "on mission" (away from Paris on official Convention business), made the Girondin leaders think it would be a good time to go on the offensive. On April 12 Guadet read from the document Marat had signed at the Jacobin Club a week earlier, and a motion was made to arrest him for sedition.[43]

With some difficulty Marat managed to get to the podium to respond. He ridiculed the accusation, explaining that his signature on the manifesto had only been a formality. He nonetheless defended its contents, saying that when Dumouriez threatened military action on behalf of the Girondins, he had clearly implicated them as accomplices in his treason. He then proposed that *both* he *and* the Girondin leaders be tried by the Revolutionary Tribunal, so all of the charges could be heard and justice could take its course. But because of the Girondins' temporary majority due to the absence of the Montagnards on mission, only the decree of accusation against Marat passed.

When the Convention's bailiffs went to take Marat into custody, however, he refused to surrender. The arrest decree was not valid, he said, because it had not been signed by the proper authorities. That small technicality could not have prevented his arrest had he not been spirited out of harm's way by a large contingent of supporters from the Mountain and the public galleries. Once outside the assembly hall, Marat disappeared into the crowd and went into hiding. It would be the last time he would have to go underground.

Although being a fugitive temporarily prevented him from participating in Convention sessions, it enhanced his status as a martyr-hero in the eyes of revolutionary Paris. That same evening the membership of the Jacobin Club angrily remonstrated against the attack on their president and Robespierre expressed strong support for Marat.[44] As an indication of how dramatically Marat's relationship with the municipal authorities had changed, on April 15 the mayor of Paris, J. N. Pache, went before the Convention to protest the arrest decree.

This time Marat's underground existence was not as onerous as it had been on previous occasions. He stayed in his own home with Simonne and was able to continue producing his journal with no difficulty. The efforts of the police to apprehend him were minimal. They went to his residence on two occasions and simply left when Simonne told them he was not there.

The motion to arrest Marat was only the Girondins' first step. The next day, April 13, they sought to formally indict him.

During the ensuing debate, when the infamous document Marat had signed was placed into evidence, 96 delegates marched to the front of the hall and added their signatures to it in solidarity with the People's Friend.[45] Robespierre declared that the attack on Marat was an attack on the Mountain as a whole. Nonetheless, with 80 Montagnards absent on mission the passage of the motion to indict was assured. With that, Marat completed a unique historical trifecta: he was the only person ordered to prison by the National Assembly, the Legislative Assembly, and the Convention.

Once again Marat actively avoided having an arrest warrant served on him, but this time there was a difference. Not wanting to unnecessarily alienate public opinion in the provinces, his response was more politically astute. Instead of denouncing the indictment and saying he would wipe his feet on it, he said he welcomed the opportunity to be heard by the Revolutionary Tribunal, and would gladly go before its judges just as soon as the official indictment was presented to him.[46]

That would not be easy for the Girondins to accomplish. Although they had succeeded in having Marat indicted in principle, the task of formulating the indictment—stating specific sedition charges based on evidence that would stand up in court—proved to be highly problematic. They did a slapdash job of it, but the depleted Convention approved the indictment anyway and on April 22 it was presented to the Revolutionary Tribunal.[47]

On April 23 Marat kept his word and turned himself in as soon as the public prosecutor, Fouquier-Tinville, notified him of the indictment. That evening the People's Friend, accompanied by a crowd of supporters that included Convention deputies, National Guard officers, municipal officials, commissioners of Parisian sections, and representatives of patriotic societies, marched off to prison. He had been allowed to choose his jail and he decided upon the Conciergerie.[48]

The following morning the same throng of supporters reassembled at the Conciergerie to escort him to the Revolutionary Tribunal. When he entered the courtroom it was already packed with his fervent partisans. Restif de la Bretonne, a well-known chronicler of the French Revolution, recorded the scene for posterity: "The accused arrived surrounded by guards; women known for their patriotism covered him with flowers and escorted him into the courtroom. There, Marat sat down where he pleased, answered as he pleased; he even questioned the judges."[49]

From the start of the proceedings when he was introduced as "the People's Friend" there could be no doubt that this was Marat's show. He was in charge and no one tried to stop him. He spoke in his own defense, and there was no prosecuting attorney. He addressed the judges without bothering to ask for the floor. The spectators were so enthusiastic in their support that Marat twice had to ask them to tone it down.[50]

Marat had no trouble demonstrating the absurdity of the charges in the hastily prepared indictment. One, for example, was based on a report in Brissot's journal that fear of Marat becoming dictator had caused a young Englishman named William Johnson to commit suicide. Marat called the best possible rebuttal witness to the stand: William Johnson! Not only was he very much alive, he also testified that he knew nothing about Marat aside from what he had read in the Girondin press.

William Johnson's famous roommate, Thomas Paine, was also called to testify.[51] Paine, one of only two foreigners elected to the Convention, was held in high regard in revolutionary France due to his outstanding role in the American Revolution and his book *The Rights of Man*, a rebuttal of Edmund Burke's condemnation of the French Revolution.[52] Unable to speak or read French, however, Paine had fallen under the sway of Girondin intellectuals. That and his strong opposition to the execution of Louis XVI had led him into conflict with Marat's political outlook. Despite his intentions, his testimony, given through translators, did not help the Girondins. According to one of Paine's biographers, after the trial he and Marat "appear to have been on neutral terms" until Marat's assassination.[53]

The trial concluded with Marat making a long speech condemning the Girondins for their treasonous complicity with Dumouriez. When he finished, the courtroom exploded in cheers. The jury unanimously acquitted "the fearless protector of the people's rights" of all charges, and a giddy celebration began.[54] Well-wishers carried him out of the courtroom on their shoulders, into the streets where a large crowd had awaited the verdict. Thousands of jubilant Parisians paraded him triumphantly through the streets as thousands more lined the streets and joined in chanting their support for Marat and the Mountain. The scene was recorded in numerous paintings and prints as "The Triumph of Marat."[55]

The Convention was in session when the spontaneous demonstration reached the assembly hall, so the crowd carried Marat through the doors and down the aisles, passing the chair of the president, who happened to be the Girondin Lasource. Marat took the floor and briefly addressed the delegates and the crowd, calling his acquittal a victory for the Convention as a whole.[56]

Marat, crowned with laurel leaves, is carried by a crowd celebrating his acquittal by the Revolutionary Tribunal. ("Triomphe de Marat," anonymous; US Library of Congress Prints and Photographs Division)

Pushing for Marat to be arrested and tried was a fatal political miscalculation on the part of the Girondins. Marat's defense provided a rallying point around which his broad and deep support could crystallize. In rallying to his side, the hostility of the city's population to the Girondins mounted to new heights.

As for the Convention, Marat's trial and triumph had rendered it more polarized than ever. All hope of reconciliation had passed; the disputes between the left and right wings could only be settled by the elimination of one by the other. By sending an elected Convention member to be tried by the Revolutionary Tribunal on capital charges the Girondins had set a precedent they would soon regret.

## THE FINAL CONFRONTATION

Throughout the month of May the struggle continued to intensify, but the Convention was paralyzed as neither the Girondins nor the Mountain were able to completely prevail over the other. A leading representative of the Plain, Bertrand Barère, engineered the establishment of a Commission of Twelve empowered to investigate and take action against any "illegalities" committed by the Paris Commune. The Mountain was adamantly opposed to this Girondin-dominated body but was unable to block its creation. The stage was thus set for a head-on collision between the Convention, still tenuously controlled by the Girondins, and the Parisian municipal government, which was in Jacobin hands.

Compounding the blunder they had made by putting Marat on trial, the Girondins had their Commission of Twelve imprison several leading Parisian agitators, including Jacques Hébert, who had become an official of the Commune, and the *Enragé* Jean Varlet. The arrests were met by a new upsurge of popular resistance. Marat accused the Girondins of trying to provoke the *sans-culottes* to violence. If so, they were playing a lethally dangerous game.

On May 25 a delegation of Parisian sections presented a petition to the Convention demanding the abolition of the

Commission of Twelve and the arrest of its members for treason. The president of the assembly, Maximin Isnard, unwisely responded by warning: "I declare, in the name of all of France, that Paris will be obliterated." Marat jumped from his seat and shouted, "Get down from the chair, president; you're dishonoring this assembly!" But Isnard would not yield. The city would be so thoroughly destroyed, he threatened, that "soon it will be necessary to search the banks of the Seine to see if Paris had ever existed!"[57] These ominous words echoed the Brunswick Manifesto, and had a similar effect. Rather than intimidating the Mountain and the *sans-culottes*, it strengthened their determination to defend the Revolution by annihilating the Girondins.

The day after Isnard's threat, Marat went to the Jacobin Club to address its members. A month earlier he had advised them to be patient, saying "The moment hasn't arrived yet; I'll let you know when it's time." Now, he said, the time had come to rise up in arms and put a decisive end to the Commission of Twelve. Robespierre's response was hesitant, but he did not attempt to counter Marat's appeal.[58] Although Marat had apparently surpassed Robespierre in popularity among the Jacobin ranks, Robespierre nonetheless continued to hold the reins of organization in his hands.

On May 27, Marat took the floor at the Convention to demand the abolition of the Commission of Twelve as an enemy of liberty and an affront to the people of Paris. No longer holding his tempestuous nature in check, he seemed virtually indistinguishable from the *Enragés*, but he nevertheless presented his case in defensive formulations. You—he was addressing the Girondins—are responsible for the intolerable rise in the price of bread. "If the patriots are driven to insurrection, it will be your doing!"[59]

Marat went to a meeting at the Évêché on the evening of May 30 where representatives of 33 Parisian sections were forming a Revolutionary Central Committee to call and lead an insurrection. What Marat did at the meeting is not known with certainty, but he reportedly called on the people to rise in arms, surround the Convention, and compel it to send the Girondin leaders before the Revolutionary Tribunal.[60] One account claims that Marat personally sounded the tocsin at City Hall in the predawn hours of May 31. Whether that is factually accurate or not, it is symbolically appropriate. Marat's political influence had certainly reached the point where he could call the people to insurrection and they would respond.

Many historians have portrayed Marat as essentially an egomaniac motivated only by a craving for personal glory, but in fact he took pains—for political reasons—to avoid credit for the key role he played in these events. He was concerned with how the Parisian uprising would be perceived by people in the rest of France, without whose support the insurrection could not succeed. He knew that he was not a popular figure in the provinces, so to allow the uprising to be depicted as his creation would play into the hands of the Revolution's enemies.

On May 31, in a morning session, the Convention was presented with a demand from a Paris Commune delegation, supported by Robespierre, that the Girondin leaders be indicted. At the same time the assembly hall was being surrounded by a massive crowd of Parisians. A showdown seemed imminent, but nothing happened.

The tension continued to mount. On the morning of June 1 the Convention received the news that the most prominent Girondin, Jean-Marie Roland, had fled and that his wife, a top Girondin leader in her own right, had been arrested. Marat warned the assembly that the anger of the people had reached the boiling point and could not be restrained if the dithering Convention failed to bring the traitorous Girondins to justice. Then he left the hall and immediately found himself surrounded by a boisterous throng who protested the Mountain's shilly-shallying and chanted, "Marat, save us!"[61]

With insurrectionary fever running especially high at City Hall, the Committee of Public Safety asked Marat to go there to try to calm down the situation. When he arrived, the president of the Commune's municipal assembly introduced him, apparently expecting him to advise the people to cool off and let their elected officials take care of the problems. Marat had other

ideas, however. Instead, he declared that the elected officials
had betrayed them and added:

> Rise up, then, sovereign people! Go to the Convention, speak your piece,
> and don't let yourselves be turned away until you get a definite response.
> After that, take action in accordance with your laws and in defense of
> your interests! That's my advice to you.[62]

Marat then decided that rather than going to the Évêché
where the Revolutionary Central Committee was preparing the
insurrection, he would go back to the Convention. There, in the
evening, with only about a hundred delegates in attendance,
a petition from the Commune was read. It demanded the
indictment of 25 Girondin leaders. Marat declared his support
for the demand.[63]

The insurrection seemed to be developing in slow motion,
but it finally came to a head on June 2. A crowd estimated at
80,000, made up of *sans-culottes* and entire units of the National
Guard, surrounded the Convention hall and blocked its exits.
More than a hundred cannons were brought into position. As
the well-organized uprising was developing outside, inside the
hall the conciliatory Barère urged the Girondins to resign. Marat
declared that their resignation was not an option; they had to
be arrested. If Dumouriez's co-conspirators were simply allowed
to leave, they would spread out across France posing as martyrs
and raising the provinces against Paris. Only patriots had the
right to resign, he said, and for emphasis he declared that he
himself would resign just as soon as the Girondins had been
brought to justice.[64]

Meanwhile, the delegates became aware of the threat that
was building up outside the hall. When it became known that
National Guardsmen were taking up positions to block the exits,
a large majority of the delegates decided to leave. To avoid the
appearance of panic, they would go out together in an orderly
manner. Almost all—including many Montagnards as well as
Girondin and Plain deputies—began to exit the hall, leaving
only Marat, Robespierre, and 20 or so others behind. They only

got as far as the gardens outside the hall, however, before being stopped by soldiers, and a tense confrontation ensured.

Marat could see great potential danger in this situation. The rest of France would never recognize the authority of a rump legislature composed only of Robespierre, himself, and a few Jacobin extremists. And what if some harebrained delegate outside in the Tuileries Gardens were to provoke a bunch of *Enragés* into touching off a bloody massacre of Convention representatives? To avoid such a disaster (he later wrote) he hurried out into the gardens and urged those who had walked out to go back inside.[65]

Some of the delegates immediately returned to their seats, and the others soon followed. At that point, the paraplegic Georges Couthon, one of Robespierre's lieutenants, was carried to the podium. Couthon moved that the Girondin leaders be arrested and his motion passed.[66] The Girondins were finished and the insurrection had triumphed.

*This was the watershed moment of the French Revolution.* The insurrection of May 31–June 2 cleared the way for the birth of the Jacobin Republic. The beginning of June 1793 marked the critical point at which the gains of 1789 and 1792 were consolidated and made irreversible. With the Girondins removed, between June 13 and July 17 the Convention passed a series of measures canceling all of the peasants' obligations without compensation—the decisive act of the revolutionary transformation from feudalism to capitalism. It put a definitive end to feudalistic restrictions on the peasants' mobility, paving the way for their transformation into a modern working class.

What the liberation of the peasantry meant for human freedom was certainly its most morally uplifting consequence, but its economic impact was even more significant in the long run. An essential prerequisite to the development of a capitalist economy is the existence of a free labor force—a pool of propertyless people who in order to survive are forced to become wageworkers. As long as the vast majority of the population is unable to leave the land, no such labor force is possible and capitalist development is sharply restricted.

That was the accomplishment of the Jacobin Republic, and Marat's importance to history was his indispensable leadership in bringing the Jacobin Republic into being.

## THE PROPHET IGNORED

On June 3, the day after the insurrection's triumph, Marat retired from active politics, as he had promised. In a letter to the Convention's president he announced that he was resigning so that the Girondins would not be able to use him as a bogeyman with which to stir up the provinces against the renewed Convention.[67] His resignation was never officially accepted by the Convention, but he simply ceased to carry out his official functions.

The political rationale he gave was sufficient motive for his resignation, but even aside from that, his illness would surely have forced him out of activity very soon. He was so sick that from June 3 until his death he only rarely left his apartment. In addition to the chronic skin condition that kept him either in bed or immersed in a medicated tub, he suffered from a debilitating lung ailment.

Despite his illness, however, he continued to publish his journal on a daily basis, but he was doing less writing and more editing. Its pages were now mostly filled with reprinted documents and letters from readers. He also continued to receive visitors on a regular basis, even while sitting in his tub. The tub was shaped like a giant shoe with a board across the top that served as writing surface. The board also protected his modesty when visitors were present, although he wore a robe while soaking in the tub.

From his tub, Marat tried to continue to play an advisory role by means of letters to the Committee of Public Safety and to the president of the Convention. To his great dismay, he found that his opinions were ignored. One week earlier his had been the most powerful voice at the Convention and now his letters were being totally disregarded.[68] He had wrongly assumed that the "purified" legislature would welcome his opinions, but with the

Girondins gone, the Montagnards no longer needed him. Some of the Mountain's leaders, especially Danton, were resentful at previously having needed Marat. Marat still had friends and followers among them, but most seemed happy to be rid of him.

Two weeks after retiring, with great effort Marat hauled himself out of his tub and his apartment and headed back to the Convention floor. He felt that otherwise his voice would not be heeded. He participated in the sessions of June 17 and 18, but it was too much for him. His comeback ended after two days and he never left his apartment again.

Marat's real influence on the course of events had reached its pinnacle on May 31–June 2, 1793, after which it rapidly declined to the vanishing point. Nevertheless, his aura continued to haunt the Convention. Even while he was still living, the People's Friend was being turned into a harmless icon—the symbolic representation of revolutionary virtue—by the very men who were scornfully ignoring his advice. After his assassination, Danton declared that the People's Friend in death would be more useful than he had been when alive. The Mountain found the authority of Marat's ghost especially valuable in fighting opponents from their left.

Marat assisted them in that effort by launching a final assault against the *Enragés* before his death. On July 4 he published a harsh denunciation of Roux, Varlet, and Leclerc as "false patriots who are more dangerous than the aristocrats and the royalists."[69] Frustration over his own diminished physical state no doubt played a role in stoking his anger, but Marat had a legitimate political point to make. In his eyes, the *Enragés* were irresponsible ultraleftists raising ultimatistic demands to mobilize the *sans-culottes* against the newborn, fragile Jacobin Republic.

Marat believed the *Enragés* were playing into the hands of the counterrevolution, and that, in his eyes, was intolerable. He knew, however, that they were giving voice to the *sans-culottes'* justifiable anger at skyrocketing food prices, which he blamed primarily on "the rapacity of the monopolists and the greed of the merchants, who are pushing the people to desperation."[70] Secondary blame would fall to the Convention if it refused to immediately take action to reduce the prices of bread and other necessary commodities. But it would be nonetheless inexcusable if the *Enragés* were to undermine the will of the people to defend the Revolution.


## THE ASSASSINATION

Marat's skin condition was aggravated by a terrible heat wave in Paris during the second week of July. As a result, he was spending even more time than usual immersed in his tub. People bearing information for the journal continued to visit, but Simonne screened them, more to protect him from exhaustion than from assassins. But on the early afternoon of July 13, it was an assassin who came calling.

Charlotte Corday, a young woman from Caen, knocked on the door and asked to speak to the People's Friend. Simonne said no, he was too ill to see anyone, so Corday left but returned a bit later with a written message for Marat, which he received without seeing her. The persistent Corday returned a third time at about 8:00 p.m. and was about to be turned away again when Marat told Simonne to let her enter. He had read her message, which indicated she had information for him regarding treasonous activities in Caen. Because Barbaroux, Guadet, Buzot, and other Girondins had set up their headquarters in Caen, Marat no doubt wanted to hear what the woman had to say.

Her story was a ruse. As soon as she was alone with Marat she drew a dagger from her blouse and stabbed him in the chest. Fatally wounded, Marat screamed for Simonne, who rushed into the room with several other people. Corday tried to flee but was quickly caught and held. An irate crowd almost lynched her on the spot, but cooler heads prevailed. She had to be questioned to determine whether she was the agent of a larger conspiracy against the Revolution.

Some documents discovered in her possession showed that she had indeed been in communication with Barbaroux and other Girondins. The papers did not prove that they conspired in, or even knew about, her plan to murder Marat. The political context of the moment, however, made it all too easy to believe that the evil deed had been ordered by the Girondin chiefs.[71]

Corday was swiftly tried and found guilty. On July 17, four days after the assassination, she was executed on the guillotine. If her purpose in killing Marat had been to further the Girondins' cause, she could hardly have been more self-deluded. A wave of public indignation inundated the Girondins and sealed their fate. The seemingly somnambulant Jacobins, whom Marat could not arouse when he was alive, suddenly sprang into life. Three months later 21 Girondins, including Brissot and Vergniaud, were sentenced to death by the Revolutionary Tribunal and were guillotined on October 30.[72] During the following months Barbaroux, Guadet and others were also captured and executed. Marat's assassination had triggered a cycle of violence that culminated in the Terror.

One of Marat's most oft-repeated prophecies—that his life would end by an assassin's hand—had come to pass. How had he been spending his final moments before the dagger struck? Appropriately, he had been editing the next day's issue of his journal, which appeared on schedule.

Despite his weakened physical state, Marat had lost none of his political acumen. His final article was a critique of the Committee of Public Safety, which Marat supported in principle, but whose personnel, aside from Louis Antoine Saint-Just, he deeply distrusted. In particular, he singled out Barère as "the most dangerous enemy of the Nation."[73] As it turned out, the opportunistic Barère would fully validate Marat's last prophecy by his role in undermining the Jacobin Republic and bringing about the Thermidorian reaction.

The date on the masthead of that final issue, number 242 of the *Publiciste de la République Française*, was July 14, 1793, the fourth anniversary of the original Bastille Day. Marat's life had ended at the age of 50. The official police inventory of his possessions listed his total monetary wealth as two foreign coins and a single *assignat* with a face value of 25 *sous*.[74]

# Conclusion
# From the Cult of Marat to
# the *Légende Noire* and Beyond

Marat's martyrdom triggered a massive outpouring of public grief throughout France, and especially in the capital. David painted his famous tribute to his friend[1] and organized a spectacular funeral pageant in Paris. The torch-lit procession wound through the streets for six hours, punctuated every five minutes by the window-rattling boom of a cannon.

The People's Friend became the object of a quasi-religious cult that compared Marat to Jesus. Portraits, busts, and medallions bearing his likeness proliferated, as did songs, poems, plays, and pageants commemorating his life and death. Newborns were named after him and Parisian streets and squares were renamed in his honor. Montmartre became Mont Marat.

Ironically, at the time of his assassination Marat had all but disappeared from the political stage. Charlotte Corday's act had revived his influence and raised it to unprecedented heights. A struggle developed over who would wield that influence as Marat's heir. The *Enragés* were the first to step forward. The final issue of Marat's *Publiciste de la République Française* was number 242; three days after the assassination Jacques Roux published a number 243 and attributed it to "Marat's ghost."[2] On July 20 Leclerc started up a new series of *Ami du peuple*.[3] Roux and Leclerc were both well aware that Marat had harshly attacked them only days before his death, but it should not be assumed that their attempt to claim his legacy was hypocritical. They no doubt sincerely believed that they alone were the only *real* revolutionaries capable of defending Marat's ideals, whether Marat himself had recognized that or not.

Père Duchesne, Hébert's journalistic alter ego, declared that Marat had appeared to him in a dream and had conferred the succession on him.[4] Hébert's claim was not without merit; aside from Robespierre no other political figure was more highly regarded by the sans-culottes. The Cordeliers Club likewise had a legitimate claim as Marat's heirs. His embalmed heart adorned the ceiling of their meeting hall, and they made genuine efforts to publish some of his previously unpublished writings. They, too, tried to resurrect his journal, but without success.

Danton's attempt to usurp Marat's political authority was more blatantly opportunistic. He cited his long record of support for Marat, which was not untruthful, but he neglected to mention his more recent attempts at distancing himself from the People's Friend. The most legitimate—and the most successful—attempt to turn Marat's memory to political advantage was that of Robespierre and the central Montagnard leaders. At the time of his assassination, Marat had indeed been solidly in their camp. At first Robespierre feared that the apotheosis of Marat might redound to the advantage of the Enragés, but their martyred comrade's posthumous influence proved too politically potent to ignore. Robespierre found it very useful in battling opponents from both the left and the right.

With regard to the threat from the right, Marat's martyrdom played a major role in the Mountain's triumph over the Girondins. The Jacobins had no difficulty implicating their right-wing rivals in the assassination of the great patriot, and making them appear to be destabilizers and fomenters of civil war. Whether Corday had been a direct Girondin agent or not hardly mattered because the assassination had obviously been a consequence of the Girondins' relentless anti-Marat campaign.

After annihilating the Girondins, Robespierre and the Jacobin leaders turned their attention to threats from the left. Left-wing agitation posed a threat to the coalition Marat had helped to forge between the sans-culottes and the Mountain. On August 8 Robespierre arranged for Simonne Évrard to address the Convention as "the widow Marat." She condemned the Enragés for trying to highjack her late husband's memory, denouncing them as "scoundrels" whose false claims to speak in Marat's name "outrage his memory and mislead the people."[5] Simonne's rebuke helped isolate the *Enragés* and contributed to their marginalization. Later in the month Jacques Roux was arrested and in January 1794 would take his own life in prison. Leclerc's *Ami du peuple* ceased publication and he would fade into obscurity.

With all of their external challengers on both the left and the right defeated, Jacobin rule apparently faced no further obstacles. Because deep social problems remained unresolved, however, the political battles between left and right soon reproduced themselves *within* the Jacobin ranks. Robespierre found himself confronted on the right by a grouping—known as the *Indulgents*—led by Danton, and on the left by a faction headed by Hébert. The *Indulgents* drew their support from the moderates in the Convention who had formerly supported the Girondins, while Hébert's base was in the radicalized Parisian sections and the Commune.[6] Despite the discord, however, Robespierre retained tenuous control.


### THE COMMITTEE OF PUBLIC SAFETY AND THE TERROR

The revolutionary regime faced a deepening crisis as internal and external threats continued to mount. Royalist rebellions were spreading in the provinces and the counterrevolutionary armies of the European Coalition drew ever closer. The climax of the Revolution was imminent. On September 5, yet another popular insurrection in Paris transformed the Committee of Public Safety, headed by Robespierre, into the *de facto* executive power of revolutionary France.

With the Revolution under siege, the Committee of Public Safety implemented the harsh policies that have become known to history as the Reign of Terror. The Jacobins, channeling the power of the *sans-culottes* and the rebellious peasants, dealt the final, mortal blows to the old regime and consolidated the Jacobin Republic.

Because it resulted in the guillotining of significant numbers of people for sabotage and treason—many of whom, no doubt, had been unjustly accused—moralizing conservatives have long pointed to the Reign of Terror as "Exhibit A" in their campaign to discredit the French Revolution as a whole. Robespierre and his fellow members of the Committee of Public Safety have frequently been portrayed as bloodthirsty paranoiacs who used wholesale executions to eliminate their opponents and intimidate the masses. The grave dangers confronting the Revolution, however, were not paranoid fantasies. Marat's assassination was a vivid reminder of the reality of the deadly conspiracies threatening revolutionary France.

But although the Terror can be justified, in a general sense, as a defensive measure necessary for the survival of the Revolution, it also gave rise to a fratricidal struggle among the revolutionaries themselves. A bitter, divisive struggle erupted between Danton's *Indulgents* and the Hébertistes. Danton made a bloc with Robespierre that succeeded in defeating the Hébertistes, but as soon as the latter were removed from the scene, Robespierre turned on the *Indulgents* and eliminated them, too. Hébert and his lieutenants were executed on March 24, 1794; Danton and his colleagues, including Camille Desmoulins, followed them to the guillotine less than two weeks later.

The extreme need for unity and security in the face of war and counterrevolution impelled Robespierre and the Committee of Public Safety to subdue the turbulent radical movement in Paris. But they could not impose control over the *sans-culottes* without suppressing the revolutionary energy that sustained their own existence. The guillotining of Hébert and other popular left-wing leaders was especially disorienting and demoralizing. The Jacobins thus paved the way for their own downfall. They could no longer take the support of the *sans-culottes* for granted. The coalition that Marat had fostered fell apart.


## THERMIDOR: RESURGENCE OF THE RIGHT

The primary justification for the Reign of Terror was the widespread fear that Paris would be annihilated and the Revolution brutally crushed by its internal and external foes.

By mid-1794 the military situation of the revolutionary armies had markedly improved. With the danger of defeat far less imminent, the extreme measures of the Terror no longer seemed necessary, eroding the *raison d'être* of the Jacobin dictatorship. The moderate wing of the Convention, reinvigorated, was able to isolate Robespierre and send him and his closest colleagues to the guillotine. The Jacobins' diehard supporters once again raised the call to insurrection, but they, too, were now isolated, and the demoralized *sans-culottes* failed to respond. The Jacobin leaders were executed on July 27, which on the new calendar created by the Revolution was 9 Thermidor. The downfall of the Jacobin Republic has thus been immortalized as *Thermidor*.

Thermidor led to a major resurgence of the right-wing elements—the remnants of the Girondins and the constitutional monarchists—who had been lying low since Marat's assassination. Seeking revenge, they unleashed a retaliatory White Terror that was far more bloody and cruel than Robespierre's.[7] But because "history is written by the victors," the White Terror has been virtually forgotten and the Jacobin Terror has come to symbolize the horrors of revolution.

"The issue of violence and terror has divided reformers and revolutionaries, as well as historians, ever since 1789," observed historian Arno Mayer. The "battle lines," he added, "hold to this day."[8] Although Marat was no longer alive at the time of the Reign of Terror, his frequent calls to revolutionary violence have often been blamed for creating the climate in which it unfolded.

Marat, however, did not relish violence for its own sake; he saw it first of all as a natural response of oppressed peoples to "the violence of the status quo,"[9] and secondly as the only possible means of defense against the violence of the counterrevolution. In the following century, Mark Twain would eloquently describe the violence of the status quo by comparing what he called the "two Reigns of Terror" in French history. "The one lasted mere months, the other had lasted a thousand years; the one inflicted death upon ten thousand persons, the other upon a hundred millions," he wrote.

A city cemetery could contain the coffins filled by that brief Terror which we have all been so diligently taught to shiver at and mourn over; but all France could hardly contain the coffins filled by that older and real Terror—that unspeakably bitter and awful Terror which none of us has been taught to see in its vastness or pity as it deserves.[10]

The Thermidorian reaction initially disguised its real nature with professions of revolutionary patriotism, and—irony of ironies—utilized the cult of Marat to do so. The revolutionary saint Marat was counterposed to the disgraced "dictator" Robespierre. That is why on September 21, 1794, with the Thermidorian reaction already well under way, the entire Convention marched in procession to install Marat's ashes in the Pantheon. This cynical manipulation of revolutionary symbolism succeeded in its aim of further confusing and demobilizing the *sans-culottes*.

Less than five months after carrying Marat's ashes to the Pantheon, the Convention made an about-face and had them removed. Hostile sources allege that the ashes were then thrown into the sewer. Whether that is true or not, the tale illustrates that by February 1795 the Thermidorians no longer needed to pretend that they were extending the Revolution. The cult of Marat was discarded and replaced by the *légende noire* of Marat the bloodthirsty monster.

The Thermidorian reaction became ever more openly reactionary. Young men from the privileged classes roamed the streets in bands called the *jeunesse dorée* ("gilded youth"), stalking and beating up left-wing activists, and destroying images of Marat. In another strange historical twist, a primary leader of these proto-fascistic gangs was a man previously known as Marat's disciple, Fréron, whose political trajectory had taken him from the extreme left to the extreme right.[11]

The rewriting of the Revolution's history was accomplished by Thermidorian scholars who drew heavily on Girondin sources. In their interpretation, Marat was a thoroughly villainous character with no redeeming qualities. It became virtually illegal, for many years, to portray Marat in a positive light. In 1847 and 1848 Constant Hilbey was jailed for republishing Marat's works, and

Alfred Bougeart spent four months in prison for publishing a biography of Marat in 1865.

Although its ideological roots have long been obvious, the Thermidorian anti-Marat campaign has never ceased to influence how the People's Friend is remembered in France and elsewhere. Mainstream historians continue, to the present day, to present

This 1871 right-wing cartoon seeks to pin the violence of the Paris Commune uprising on Marxists and on Marat's memory. Karl Marx, firebrand in hand, yells at the image of Marat, "Va donc, Berquin!" which means, in rough translation, *OK, Pollyanna, do something!* ("Va donc, Berquin," drawn by Cham [pseudonym of Amédée-Charles-Henry de Noé]. Published in *Le Charivari*, June 18, 1871.)

his story as a cautionary tale demonstrating the horrors of radicalism and the futility of social revolution. Later generations of revolutionaries, however, from Babeuf to Blanqui to Raspail, and from the Paris Commune of 1871 to the Russian Revolution of 1917, looked to Marat as a hero and guiding spirit.

Oddly enough, even Karl Marx and Frederick Engels seem to have allowed themselves to be influenced by the Thermidorian distortions. In *The Holy Family* (1844) they cite the *Enragés*, Babeuf, and Buonarroti as revolutionary antecedents, but neglect to mention Marat. In *The Eighteenth Brumaire of Louis Napoleon* (1852), Marx hails Danton, Desmoulins, Robespierre, Saint-Just, and Napoleon as "heroes" of the Revolution, again omitting Marat. Engels acknowledged, after Marx's death, that it was not until the 1865 publication of Bougeart's biography that they had come to appreciate Marat's role in the Revolution.[12]

Marat's memory was lovingly upheld by his widow and his younger sister, Albertine. After the assassination Albertine left her Geneva home and moved to Paris, where she and Simonne would share an apartment and an impoverished existence in the shadow of the *légende noire* until Simonne's death three decades later. Albertine would then continue the lonely vigil for another 17 years, outliving her illustrious sibling by almost half a century.

## ASSESSING MARAT'S HISTORICAL IMPORTANCE

Many historians have dismissed Marat's contributions to the French Revolution as essentially irrelevant. His fame, in this interpretation, was more a matter of image than substance. The narrative presented in this biography indicates, to the contrary, that he was an effective political leader whose actions drove the Revolution forward.

His first and most consistent role was that of journalist. The products of his pen did not simply reflect the current moods of the masses. His political positions were always in advance of his readership, and he was obliged to continually win it over to his opinions at every stage of the revolutionary process. Although changes in mass political consciousness rarely occurred at a pace fast enough to satisfy Marat, his main audience, the Parisian *sans-culottes*, eventually followed his lead throughout his career.

As a political strategist and tactician, Marat showed himself to be the equal of any of history's most effective revolutionary leaders. He consistently and accurately identified the central issues of the moment, as well as the main line of the Revolution's development, and tirelessly hammered them into his readers' consciousness. His early recognition of the reactionary essence of the Girondins' appeal for an international military crusade is a prime example. Marat's most significant strategic move was the "new course" he embarked upon after the insurrection of August 10, 1792, which aimed at constructing an alliance of Jacobins and *sans-culottes*. That coalition was essential to the process of consolidating the Revolution's gains, and no one was more important in bringing it into being than Marat.

Marat's tactical acumen—his sense of *what to do next* at every moment during the upheavals of a revolutionary situation—was repeatedly demonstrated by his uncanny ability to provoke the authorities while evading arrest. That he was able to stay a step ahead of the police of successive regimes *for several years* means that his success cannot be attributed to good luck. And when the time came that he no longer had to evade the authorities, his tactical prowess remained evident in his ability to continuously force the Convention onto the grounds of *his* agenda.

Marat's tactical masterpiece was the conversion of his own trial into a decisive triumph over his Girondin prosecutors. His decision to evade arrest until a formal indictment had been brought against him was a critical one. Had he allowed himself to be imprisoned on the initial vague decree of accusation, the Girondins could have stalled and left him to rot in jail. If they had succeeded in that, they could well have regained the political momentum they needed to block the consolidation of the Jacobin Republic.

The most spectacular example of Marat's tactical genius, however, was his intervention in the events that resulted in the insurrection of May 31–June 2. At the beginning of April he had warned the overzealous *sans-culottes* against prematurely rising in revolt. At the end of May, when he felt the time had come, he embarked upon a whirlwind of agitational activity—at the *Hôtel de Ville*, at the Convention, and in the streets—injecting an element of clarity into an otherwise confused mass movement.

The balance sheet of Marat's political leadership, however, has one significant entry on the deficit side. He did not organize his followers into a political party. Both Robespierre and Brissot, by contrast, created solid, loyal, organized followings they could count on to follow their lead in crucial situations. Marat showed that he recognized the need for cadre political formations, but he did not create any himself. Although hailed as "father of the fraternal societies," it was strictly an honorary title; none actually looked to him directly for leadership. The difference between Marat and Robespierre in this regard is best exemplified by the fact that Marat might well not have been elected to the Convention at all had Robespierre not instructed the Jacobins under his command to vote for the People's Friend.

Marat's failure to create a party owed to his conviction that being at the head of a party would compromise his political independence. When the Girondins accused the Mountain of being controlled by a "*Maratiste* party," Marat angrily avowed that no such party had ever existed. His only "party," he declared, was "the people."[13] By the time he decided to subordinate himself to the Mountain, however, he may well have come to regret the lack of a *Maratiste* party, but it was too late—the parties of the Revolution had already been formed.

That Marat's role in the Revolution was not as central as Robespierre's is evidenced by the fact that the Revolution continued to deepen in the wake of Marat's assassination, while Robespierre's defeat and execution immediately resulted in its definitive reversal.

## CONTRAFACTUAL MUSINGS

*What if* Marat had not been assassinated? Would the Revolution have had a different outcome? *What if* he had lived to experience the Reign of Terror? Would he have supported it?

The first of these hypothetical problems offers but one realistic solution: No, it is virtually unimaginable that Marat's continued presence on the scene could have significantly altered the course of the Revolution. Even if his debilitating illness had miraculously ceased to afflict him, the tide of counterrevolution in 1794 was too powerful for any individual leader, no matter how talented, to withstand. At most, he might have helped sustain the Jacobin–*sans-culotte* coalition a little longer, which could possibly have postponed the triumph of the reaction to a month other than Thermidor.

On the other hand, it is also easy to imagine Marat being guillotined with Hébert and the other partisans of the *sans-culottes* in March 1794, or escaping that fate by once again disappearing into the underground. Unfortunately for Marat, the kind of social revolution he sought—elimination of the immense gulf between rich and poor—was an impossible dream in the late eighteenth century. The fall of Robespierre, the failure of Babeuf's Conspiracy of Equals, the rise of Bonaparte, and the Bourbon Restoration all testify to that. After the insurrection of May 31–June 2, there was no further role for Marat to play. Charlotte Corday unwittingly helped him exit the stage with the best timing he could have hoped for.

As for how Marat would have reacted to the Reign of Terror, the traditional view assumes that he would have enthusiastically supported it, but that is based on the fallacy of the *légende noire*. Marat had consistently advocated a provisional revolutionary dictatorship of the kind embodied by the Committee of Public Safety, and there can be little doubt that he would have approved of Robespierre heading it up, but beyond that the picture is far less clear. It is safe to assume that he would have joined the fight against the *Indulgents*, but not that he would have acquiesced in the guillotining of Danton and Desmoulins. It is almost unthinkable that he would have supported the liquidation of the Hébertistes and the Cordeliers leaders who had been his closest collaborators. Exactly how Marat would have reacted to these events, and how they would have affected his personal fate, is of course unknowable.

And finally, *what if* Marat were to return today? What would he think of the state of our planet in the second decade of the twenty-first century? He could read in the history books that the Great French Revolution—*his* Revolution—is recognized as the watershed event in the making of the modern world.

"*But what did it accomplish?*" he might ask.

"It rid France of a parasitic class whose right to rule was based upon aristocratic birthright and traditional privilege."

"*Is that all?*"

"It established legal and political equality, which then spread throughout much of Europe and the world."

"*Legal and political equality? What about economic and social equality?*"

"No, the situation in that regard is even worse than you remember it. Today, despite two centuries of mind-boggling technological progress, a handful of billionaires control most of the Earth's resources while billions of people remain mired in hunger, disease, oppression, and grinding poverty."

Marat would surely be shocked and dismayed to learn that after more than 200 years his struggle for social revolution had lost none of its relevance and urgency. Where is the People's Friend now, when we need him?

# Notes

## PREFACE

1. Jean Massin, *Marat* (Paris: Club français du livre, 1970); Olivier Coquard, *Marat* (Paris: Fayard, 1993).
2. Louis Gottschalk, *Jean Paul Marat: A Study in Radicalism* (Chicago: University of Chicago Press, 1967); Clifford D. Conner, *Jean Paul Marat: Scientist and Revolutionary* (Atlantic Highlands, NJ: Humanities Press, 1997).

## INTRODUCTION

1. Victor Hugo, *Œuvres complètes* (Paris, 1910), vol. XV, 524. (All translations from the French are by the present author unless otherwise noted.)
2. The revisionist school of thought was initiated by Alfred Cobban's "Myth of the French Revolution" lecture in May 1954; see Cobban, *The Social Interpretation of the French Revolution* (Cambridge: Cambridge University Press, 1964). For Lefebvre's interpretation, see especially *The French Revolution* (New York: Columbia University Press, 1962).
3. Sidney L. Phipson, *Marat: His Career in England and France Before the Revolution* (London: Methuen, 1924), 16, 48, 86.
4. Ibid., v.
5. Ibid., 134.
6. Ibid., 83.
7. *Correspondance*, 1–2.
8. See, for example, J. M. Thompson, *Leaders of the French Revolution* (Oxford: Basil Blackwell, 1988), 167.
9. Robert Darnton, "Marat n'a pas été un voleur," *Annales historiques de la Révolution française* 38 (1966), 447–50.

10. Douglas McKie, *Antoine Lavoisier, Scientist, Economist, Social Reformer* (New York: Schuman, 1952), 318.

11. Charles W. Burr, "Jean Paul Marat, Physician, Revolutionary, Paranoaic," *Annals of Medical History* III (1919), 248–61.

12. See, for example, Norman Hampson, *Will and Circumstance: Montesquieu, Rousseau and the French Revolution* (Norman: University of Oklahoma Press, 1983), 119.

13. Burr, "Jean Paul Marat," 260.

14. Ibid., 259.

15. Ibid., 257.

16. L. F. Maury, *L'Ancienne Académie des Sciences* (Paris: Didier, 1864), 174.

17. For a thorough account of Marat's scientific career, go to this website: www.MaratScience.com

18. In addition to Louis Gottschalk's biography, see also Gérard Walter, *Marat* (Paris: Albin Michel, 1933).

## CHAPTER 1

1. Fabre d'Eglantine, *Portrait of Marat* (Paris: Maradan, 1794).

2. The definitive source of information on the Mara family is Charlotte Goëtz, *Marat en famille: La saga des Mara(t)*, 2 volumes (Bruxelles: Pôle Nord, 2001).

3. Marat's letter of May 14, 1776, in Darnton, "Marat n'a pas été un voleur."

4. The text of the declaration is in Alfred Bougeart, *Marat, l'ami du people* (Paris: Libraire Internationale, 1865), vol. I, 350.

5. "A Portrait of the People's Friend, Drawn by Himself" in *JRF*, no. 98, January 14, 1793. The two quotations that follow are from the same source.

6. Marat, *Les Aventures du jeune comte Potowski* (Paris: Chlendowski, 1848). A "bicentennial edition" was published in 1989 (Monaco: Renaudot, 1989).

7. Lettre à Roume de Saint-Laurent (November 20, 1783), *Correspondance*, 23–44.

8. Ibid.

9. *Gazette de politique et de literature*, May 5, 1777.

10. Diderot, *Eléments de physiologie*, in *Œuvres complètes* (Paris: Garnier, 1875), vol. XI, 378.

11. *AP* no. 455, May 11, 1791.

12. *PRF* no. 147, November 19, 1793.

13. It was reported as hearsay by Jacques Pierre Brissot, who had become Marat's bitter enemy. See Jacques Pierre Brissot de Warville, *Mémoires, 1754–1793* (Paris: Picard et Fils, 1912), vol. I, 196.

14. See the letters to Marat from Lyttleton, Collignon and La Rochette in *Correspondance*, 45–50.

15. Gottschalk, *Jean Paul Marat*, 19.

16. Massin, *Marat*, 39.

17. For an in-depth analysis of the antecedents of Marat's ideology, particularly with regard to the British commonwealth tradition, see Rachel Hammersley, "Jean-Paul Marat's *The Chains of Slavery* in Britain and France, 1774–1833," *The Historical Journal*, vol. 48, no. 3 (September 2005).

18. Marat, *Chains of Slavery*, 210.

19. Ibid., 68.

20. Ibid., 108.

21. Ibid., 124.

22. Ibid., 68.

23. Hammersley demonstrates not only that Marat utilized the ideas he formulated in *Chains of Slavery* in France between 1789 and 1793, but that others continued to do so for several decades after his death.

24. Marat, *Plan de legislation criminelle*. There is a modern edition (Paris: Aubier Montaigne, 1974).

25. *AP* no. 169, 22 July 1790.

26. Marat, *Plan de legislation criminelle*, 59.

27. Ibid., 62.

## CHAPTER 2

1. Marat, *An Essay on Gleets*, in *Reprint of Two Tracts by Jean Paul Marat, M.D.*, ed., James Blake Bailey (London: Percival & Co., 1891).

2. The text of Marat's diploma is in F. Chèvremont, *Jean-Paul Marat* (Paris, 1880), 363–5.

3. For one example, see William Buchan, *Domestic Medicine; or, The family physician* (Edinburgh, 1769).

4. *An Essay on Gleets* (October 1769) and *An Enquiry into the Nature, Cause and Cure of a Singular Disease of the Eyes* (January 1773), both in *Reprint of Two Tracts by Jean Paul Marat, M.D.*

5. See the discussion of Marat's degree in Jean François Lemaire, "Le Dr. Jean-Paul Marat," in *MHdS*.

6. *Gazette de Santé*, November 13, 1777, 189–90.

7. Gottschalk, *Jean Paul Marat*, 9.

8. Quoted by Robert Darnton, *Literary Underground of the Old Regime* (Cambridge, Mass.: Harvard University Press, 1982), 26–7. Darnton's source: Lenoir papers, Bibliothèque Municipal d'Orleans, ms. 1423.

9. *Gazette de Santé*, January 1, 1778.

10. David M. Vess, *Medical Revolution in France, 1789–1796* (Gainesville: University Presses of Florida, 1975), 17.

11. Ibid.

12. Lemaire, "Le Dr. Jean-Paul Marat," *MHdS*, 22.

13. See the extensive discussion of "Jacobin science" in Marshall Clagett, *Critical Problems in the History of Science* (Madison: University of Wisconsin Press, 1959).

14. Marat's three main works on fire, light, and electricity were, respectively, *Recherches physiques sur le feu* (Paris: Jombert, 1780), *Découvertes sur la lumière* (Paris: Jombert, 1780), and *Recherches physiques sur l'électricité* (Paris: Clousier, 1782).

15. Marat's three main works on fire, light, and electricity were translated by Christian Ehrenfriend Weigel (Leipzig, S. L. Crusius, 1782–84).

16. See Norman Bernard Mandelbaum, "Jean-Paul Marat: The Rebel as Savant," (unpublished dissertation, Columbia University, 1977), 511–13.

17. Jean Baptiste Lamarck, *Réfutation de la théorie pneumatique* (Paris: Agasse, 1796); le comte de Lacépède, *Essai sur l'électricité naturelle et artificielle* (Paris: Impr. de Monsieur, 1781); Baltazar Georges Sage, *Institutions de physique* (Paris, 1811).

18. Johann Wolfgang von Goethe, *Zur Farbenlehre* (Tübingen, 1810).

19. See Mandelbaum, "Rebel as Savant," 382.

20. Marat, *Mémoire sur l'électricité médicale* (Paris: Méquignon, 1784).

21. This essay and the two for the Academy of Lyon were published in Marat's *Mémoires académiques* (Paris: Méquignon, 1788).

22. See Mandelbaum, "Rebel as Savant," 369–74.

23. See especially Claudius Roux, *Marat et l'Académie de Lyon* (Lyon: M. Audin, 1923).

24. Olivier Coquard, "Marat et les Académies de province," in *MHdS*, 65–93.

25. Marat, *Pamphlets*, 255–96.

26. For Marat's relationship with Franklin, see their correspondence from 1779 to 1783 in *Revue historique de la Révolution*, vol. III, 1912, 353–61, and Marat, *Correspondance*, 81–2.

27. *Registres de l'Académie des Sciences*, 1779, 97–100. Marat published it at the beginning of his *Découvertes de M. Marat sur le feu, l'électricité, et la lumière* (Paris: Clousier, 1779).

28. Marat published this report, followed by his own comments, at the beginning of his *Découvertes sur la lumière*.

29. C. C. Gillispie, *Science and Polity in France at the End of the Old Regime* (Princeton: Princeton University Press, 1980), 307–8.

30. Ibid., 328.

31. Ibid., 320–1.

32. Isaac Newton, *Optique*, traduit de l'anglais par Jean-Paul Marat (Paris: Christian Bourgois, 1989).

33. See Augustin Cabanès, *Marat Inconnu* (Paris: A. Michel, 1911), 91, 506–8.

34. For example, Gottschalk, *Jean Paul Marat*, 30–1.

35. Marat, *l'Ami du Peuple, aux amis de la Patrie*, in *Pamphlets*, 309–12; *Les Charlatans modernes*, in *Pamphlets*, 292.

36. Lettre au Président de l'Assemblée Nationale (May 1790), *Correspondance*, 142.

## CHAPTER 3

1. *Correspondance*, 96.

2. The precise identification of Marat's skin disease has long been a subject of speculation. In 1900, Ernest Belfort Bax declared that

there is "no doubt whatever that it was the skin disease known as pruritus" (Ernest Belfort Bax, *Jean Paul Marat: The People's Friend* [London: Grant Richards, 1900], ch. 5). In 1979, J. E. Jelinek identified it as *dermatitis herpetiformis* (Jelinek, "Jean-Paul Marat: The differential diagnosis of his skin disease," *American Journal of Dermatopathology*, vol. 1, no. 3 [1979], 251–2). Other guesses have included scrofula, skin cancer, and psoriasis.

3. *Correspondance*, 142.
4. This is the "Lefebvre Thesis." See Georges Lefebvre, *The Coming of the French Revolution* (Princeton, NJ: Princeton University Press, 1947).
5. *Offrande à la patrie*, in *Pamphlets*, 1–35.
6. Ibid., 21, 31.
7. Ibid., 22.
8. Ibid., 15, 28.
9. Ibid., 20.
10. *Supplément de l'Offrande à la patrie*, in *Pamphlets*, 37–70.
11. Ibid., 49–50.
12. Ibid., 39–40.
13. Ibid., 70.
14. *AP* no. 36, November 12, 1789.
15. Ibid.
16. *AP* no. 20, September 30, 1789.
17. See Massin, *Marat*, 91.
18. According to one study of the printing business at the time of the Revolution, "The lower limit of economic viability for a periodical in the eighteenth century seems to have been a press run of about 300 copies" (Harvey Chisick, "Production, Distribution and Readership of a Conservative Journal of the Early French Revolution: The *Ami du Roi* of the Abbé Royou," *Memoirs of the American Philosophical Society*, vol. 198 [Philadelphia, 1992], 19). Marat's press runs were far higher, meaning that he had the possibility of doing much better than merely breaking even. Furthermore, although there are no figures available to directly determine the profitability of Marat's journal, another journal, "comparable in format and circulation to *L'Ami du peuple*" (Coquard, *Marat*, 464), earned an annual profit of about 62,000 livres (Gilles Feyel, "Les frais d'impression et de diffusion de la

presse parisienne entre 1789 et 1792," *La Révolution du journal*, 1788–1794, Centre national de la recherche scientifique [CNRS] [Paris, 1989]). Marat's personal "net worth" at the time of his death was virtually nil, so if the paper's income was exceeding its expenses, he was most likely putting the surplus toward expanding his printing capacity.

19. J.-B.-C. Delisle de Sales, *Essai sur le journalisme depuis 1735 jusqu'à l'an 1800* (Paris: impr. de Colas, 1811), 96–7.

20. Chisick, "Production, Distribution and Readership of a Conservative Journal," 66.

21. Lise Andries, "Radicalism and the Book in Paris During the French Revolution," CNRS (Paris, 2006).

22. *AP* no. 11, September 21, 1789.

23. Marat, *La Constitution ou Projet de déclaration des droits de l'homme et du citoyen* (Paris: Buisson, 1789).

24. Ibid., 7.

25. Ibid., 13–15.

26. *Actes*, vol. I, 206.

27. George Rudé, *The Crowd in the French Revolution* (Oxford: Oxford University Press, 1972), 178. Rudé's book remains the best source of information on the *sans-culottes*. Another worthy source is Albert Soboul, *The Sans-Culottes* (Princeton, NJ: Princeton University Press, 1980).

28. *AP* no. 667, July 7, 1792.

29. *Actes*, vol. II, 69.

30. Lettre aux représentants de la Commune (September 25, 1789), *Correspondance*, 104.

31. *Actes*, vol. II, 103–4.

32. *AP* no. 25, October 5, 1789.

33. See Rudé, *The Crowd in the French Revolution*, 76.

34. *AP* no. 29, November 5, 1789.

35. *AP* no. 34, November 10, 1789.

36. *AP* no. 35, November 11, 1789.

37. Ibid.

38. *Actes*, vol. II, 202.

39. *AP* no. 27, October 7, 1789.

40. *Le Père Duchesne* no. 82, September 30, 1791.

41. *AP* no. 70, December 11, 1789.
42. *AP* no. 71, December 19, 1789.
43. Ibid.
44. *Appel à la Nation*, ca. April 1790, in *Pamphlets*, 122.
45. *AP* no. 83, December 31, 1789.
46. Ibid.
47. *Actes*, vol. III, 458.
48. *Dénonciation contre Necker*, in *Pamphlets*, 97.
49. See *Actes*, vol. III, 517, 520–5, 528, 540–51.
50. *Appel à la Nation*, in *Pamphlets*, 121–64. The other two pamphlets were *Lettre sur l'ordre judiciaire* (*Correspondance*, 135–40) and *Nouvelle dénonciation contre Necker* (*Pamphlets*, 165–96).
51. *Appel à la Nation*, in *Pamphlets*, 160–1.
52. Ibid., 155.
53. *Soc. Jac.*, vol. V, 226.
54. For an extensive list of printers and booksellers that produced and distributed *Ami du peuple* at one time or another, see Coquard, *Marat*, 256–8.
55. *AP* no. 170, July 23, 1790.
56. Lettre à Camille Desmoulins (May 1791), *Correspondance*, 208. Also, *AP* no. 455, May 11, 1791.
57. Lettre à Camille Desmoulins (June 24, 1790), *Correspondance*, 151–3.
58. *AP* no. 474, May 30, 1791. Besides Desmoulins and Fréron, the others were Pierre Jean Audouin, *Journal universel*; Louis Marie Prudhomme, *Les Révolutions de Paris*; and Pierre François Robert, *Mercure national*.
59. *Rév. France/Brabant* no. 69.
60. Lettre à Camille Desmoulins (May 1791), *Correspondance*, 203.
61. *Correspondance*, 153–8. Marat published a revised version of this article in *AP* no. 149, June 30, 1790.
62. The article, from *AP* no. 147, June 28, 1790, was a denunciation of Lafayette.
63. *AP* no. 149, June 30, 1790.
64. Rudé, *The Crowd in the French Revolution*, 178.
65. The numerical proportion of wageworkers among the "working classes" in late-eighteenth-century Paris is difficult to determine

(not least because the ways workers gained their livelihoods are often difficult to categorize), but it was certainly much smaller than it would become during and after the Industrial Revolution. One reasonable estimate put the number of "wage-earners and their families" in Paris in 1791 at slightly less than 300,000 (Rudé, *The Crowd in the French Revolution*, 17), which would suggest that wageworkers themselves accounted for a small fraction of the city's population. With regard to the wageworkers' social weight, however, their lack of concentration and organization was more significant than their numerical strength. They were scattered among tens of thousands of small workplaces and prevented by law and tradition from organizing unions or other types of associations to defend their interests.

66.  *AP* no. 156, July 7, 1790.
67.  *Pamphlets*, 197–200.
68.  *Le Junius Français*, no. 1, June 2, 1790.
69.  See, for example, "Address to All the Passive Citizens of the Capital," *AP* no. 172, July 25, 1790.
70.  *Pamphlets*, 201–9.
71.  Ibid.
72.  *Rév. France/Brabant* no. 37.
73.  Quoted in *Œuvres*, 132–3.
74.  In *Pamphlets*, 219–27, 229–35, and 237–45, respectively.
75.  *Le Junius Français*, no. 10, June 13, 1790.
76.  *AP* no. 198, August 22, 1790.
77.  *AP* no. 200, August 24, 1790.
78.  *Pamphlets*, 244.
79.  *Rév. France/Brabant* no. 41.
80.  *Rév. France/Brabant* no. 47.
81.  *AP* no. 207, August 31, 1790, and no. 278, November 12, 1790.
82.  *AP* no. 224, September 18, 1790.
83.  *AP* no. 374, February 17, 1791.
84.  *AP* no. 342, January 16, 1791.
85.  *AP* no. 384, February 27, 1791.
86.  See Desmoulins's account in *Rév. France/Brabant* no. 63.
87.  *AP* no. 419, April 4, 1791.

88. The historian J. M. Thompson called Marat "the one man unkind and clear-sighted enough to denounce [Mirabeau] when he died" (*Leaders of the French Revolution* [Oxford: Basil Blackwell, 1988], 39).
89. *AP* no. 496, June 21, 1791.
90. *AP* no. 503, June 27, 1791.
91. *Le Père Duchesne* no. 60, July 3, 1791.

## CHAPTER 4

1. *AP* no. 524, July 20, 1791.
2. *AP* no. 549, September 8, 1791.
3. *AP* nos. 555 and 557, September 20 and 22, 1791.
4. *AP* no. 555, September 20, 1791.
5. *AP* no. 556, September 21, 1791.
6. *AP* nos. 557, 558, and 559 (September 22, 23, and 25, 1791).
7. *AP* no. 560, September 27, 1791.
8. Charavay, *Assemblée Électorale de Paris* (Paris, 1890), vol. II, 168.
9. *AP* no. 568, October 6, 1791.
10. Rudé, *The Crowd in the French Revolution*, 102.
11. *AP* no. 667, July 7, 1792.
12. *AP* no. 582, October 25, 1791.
13. *AP* no. 622, December 10, 1791.
14. *AP* nos. 625 and 626, December 14 and 15, 1791.
15. See *AP* no. 627, April 12, 1792.
16. *AP* no. 648, May 3, 1792.
17. Robespierre, *Œuvres* (Paris: Presses Universitaires de France, 1958), vol. IX, 80.
18. *AP* no. 628, April 13, 1792.
19. *AP* no. 634, April 19, 1792.
20. *AP* no. 639, April 24, 1792.
21. Ibid.
22. *AP* no. 646, "April 31," 1792. April 31 was a typographical error in the masthead; the issue appeared on May 1. Marat did not refer

directly to the death of General Dillon until *AP* no. 649, May 6, 1792.

23. *Arch. Parl.*, vol. XLII, 706–14.

24. This was intended for publication as a placard on July 13, but Marat was unable to find a printer willing to handle it. It was published a few days later in *AP* nos. 674 and 675, July 18 and 20, 1792.

25. *JRF* no. 33, October 27, 1792. The letter was printed by Marat, but it was authenticated by Barbaroux in his *Mémoires* (Paris: Baudouin Frères, 1822), 62.

26. *AP* no. 634, April 19, 1792.

27. Women did not win the right to vote in France until after World War II.

28. Marat would be forced into hiding again in November 1792 and April 1793 but for only a few days on both occasions.

29. *L'Ami du peuple aux français patriotes*, in *Œuvres*, 216.

30. Ibid., 218–9.

31. *AP* no. 681, August 21, 1792.

32. *Marat, l'ami du peuple, aux braves Parisiens*, in *Pamphlets*, 301–3.

33. *Marat, l'ami du peuple, à ses concitoyens*, in *Pamphlets*, 305–8.

34. *JRF* no. 12, October 6, 1792.


## CHAPTER 5

1. In *Pamphlets*, 305–8, 309–12, 313–17, and 325–34.

2. *Marat, l'Ami du Peuple, aux Amis de la Patrie*, in *Pamphlets*, 309–12.

3. Ibid.

4. Robespierre, *Œuvres*, vol. VIII, 463 (note).

5. Charavay, *Assemblée Électorale de Paris*, vol. III, 123.

6. *Arch. Parl.* (April 10, 1793), vol. LXI, 525.

7. *JRF* no. 1, September 25, 1792.

8. *Soc. Jac.*, vol. IV, 378 and 383.

9. *AP* no. 667, July 7, 1792. Emphasis added.

10. *Soc. Jac.* (session of December 23, 1792), vol. IV, 613.

11. *Mon. univ.* no. 271, September 27, 1792.

12. Ibid.
13. Ibid.
14. Ibid.
15. *JRF* no. 20, October 14, 1792.
16. *JRF* no. 60, November 29, 1792.
17. *Soc. Jac.*, vol. IV, 383–4.
18. Ibid., 387.
19. Ibid., 393.
20. See Marat's report to the Jacobin Club on October 17, 1792: *Soc. Jac.*, vol. IV, 399–401. See also Marat's account of the confrontation with Dumouriez in *JRF* no. 27, October 21, 1792.
21. *Mon. univ.* no. 293, October 19, 1792.
22. *Mon. univ.* no. 300, October 26, 1792.
23. *JRF* no. 33, October 27, 1792.
24. *Mon. univ.* no. 343, December 8, 1792.
25. *Mon. univ.* no. 20, January 20, 1793.
26. *JRF* no. 105, January 23, 1793.
27. *Mon. univ.* no. 45, February 14, 1793.
28. Ibid.
29. Marat's denunciation of ultraradicalism can perhaps bear comparison with Lenin's harsh polemics against what he called "infantile leftwing communists." V. I. Lenin, *"Left-Wing" Communism, An Infantile Disorder* (Moscow, 1920).
30. *JRF* no. 81, December 22, 1792.
31. *JRF* no. 133, February 25, 1793.
32. P. J. B. Buchez and P. C. Roux, *Histoire parlementaire de la Révolution française* (Paris, 1834–38), vol. XXV, 74–5. See also, *Arch. Parl.*, vol. LX, 125.
33. Buchez and Roux, *Histoire parlementaire*, 75.
34. On March 14, 1793 Marat's daily periodical underwent a final name change, from *Journal de la République Française (JRF)* to *Publiciste de la République Française (PRF)*.
35. *Soc. Jac.*, vol. V, 108.
36. *Mon. univ.* no. 90, March 31, 1793.
37. *Mon. univ.* no. 91, April 1, 1793.
38. *Soc. Jac.*, vol. V, 117.
39. See Dumouriez's letters in *Mon. univ.* no. 95, April 5, 1793.

40. Quoted by Massin, *Marat*, 256.
41. *Soc. Jac.*, vol. V, 125–6.
42. Ibid., 126–8.
43. *Arch. Parl.* (April 12, 1793), vol. LXI, 637–44.
44. *Soc. Jac.*, vol. V, 133.
45. *Mon. univ.* no. 107, April 17, 1793.
46. Lettre à la Convention (April 17, 1793), *Correspondance*, 251–6. Also, *PRF* no. 171, April 18, 1793.
47. *Arch. Parl.* (April 20, 1793), vol. LXIII, 29–31.
48. Marat announced his surrender in *PRF* no. 176, April 23, 1793.
49. Restif de la Bretonne, *Les Nuits de Paris* (New York: Random House, 1964), 336. Translation by L. Asher and E. Fertig.
50. Buchez and Roux, *Histoire parlementaire*, vol. XXVI, 114. The transcript of the proceedings is reproduced on pages 114–30.
51. Bernard Vincent, *Thomas Paine ou la Religion de la liberté* (Paris: Aubier, 1987), 272–9.
52. Edmund Burke, *Reflections on the French Revolution* (London, 1790).
53. A. J. Ayer, *Thomas Paine* (Chicago: University of Chicago Press, 1988), 124.
54. Buchez and Roux, *Histoire parlementaire*, vol. XXVI, 129.
55. Six are reproduced in Coquard, *Marat*, 515–6.
56. *Mon. univ.* no. 116, April 26, 1793.
57. *Mon. univ.* no. 147, May 27, 1793.
58. *Soc. Jac.*, vol. V, 207–8.
59. *Mon. univ.* no. 148, May 28, 1793.
60. Alphonse Esquiros, *Histoire des Montagnards* (Paris: Lecou, 1847), 350–3. Esquiros said his account was based on notes written by Marat that had been given to him by Marat's sister, Albertine Marat.
61. *PRF* no. 209, June 6, 1793.
62. Buchez and Roux, *Histoire parlementaire*, vol. XXVII, 356–7. See also, *Mon. univ.* no. 155, June 4, 1793.
63. *Arch. Parl.*, vol. LXV, 689.
64. *Mon. univ.* no. 156, June 5, 1793.
65. *PRF* no. 209, June 6, 1793.

66. *Arch. Parl.*, vol. LXV, 706. See also, *Mon. univ.* no. 156, June 5, 1793.

67. Lettre à la Convention (June 3, 1793), *Correspondance*, 259–60.

68. Lettre à Thuriot (July 5, 1793), *Correspondance*, 275. Also, *Arch. Parl.*, vol. LXVIII, 278.

69. *PRF* no. 233, July 4, 1793.

70. *PRF* no. 224, June 23, 1793.

71. See Chabot's initial report to the Convention on the inquiry into Marat's assassination and the discussion on it in *Arch. Parl.* (July 14, 1793), vol. LXVIII, 710 et seq. (especially 728–9).

72. One of them, Charles Eléonore Valazé, committed suicide before he could be executed.

73. *PRF* no. 242, July 14, 1793.

74. "Procès-verbal d'apposition et de levée des scellés chez Jean-Paul Marat, 13–25 juillet 1793." In François Chevremont, *Jean-Paul Marat, esprit politique accompagné de sa vie scientifique, politique et privée* (Paris, 1880), vol. II, 503–4. The *sou* was a French coin worth one-twentieth of a *livre*. According to George Rudé, "In Paris in 1789, a labourer's daily wage might be 20 to 30 *sous*, a journeyman mason might earn 40 *sous*, and a carpenter or locksmith 50 *sous*" (Rudé, *The Crowd in the French Revolution*, 21).

## CONCLUSION

1. Jacques Louis David's masterpiece *La Mort de Marat*, depicting the assassinated Marat lying lifeless in his tub, has become one of the most familiar images of the French Revolution.

2. *Le Publiciste de la République Française, par l'Ombre de Marat*, July 16, 1793.

3. *L'Ami du peuple, par Leclerc*, July 20, 1793.

4. See *Père Duchesne* nos. 264, 268, and 275.

5. *Arch. Parl.*, vol. LXX, 527–8.

6. See Morris Slavin's detailed study, *The Hébertistes to the Guillotine* (Baton Rouge: Louisiana State University Press, 1994).

7.  See Georges Lefebvre, *The Thermidorians* (New York: Vintage, 1964), Chapter 7.

8.  Arno J. Mayer, *The Furies: Violence and Terror in the French and Russian Revolutions* (Princeton, NJ: Princeton University Press, 2000), 95.

9.  The "violence of the status quo" has been defined in part as "the agony of millions who in varying degrees suffer hunger, poverty, ill-health, lack of education, non-acceptance by their fellow men." (Jim Bristol, *Non-violence: Not First for Export* [American Friends Service Committee, 1972]).

10. Mark Twain, *A Connecticut Yankee in King Arthur's Court* (1889).

11. See François Gendron, *The Gilded Youth of Thermidor* (Montreal and Kingston: McGill-Queen's University Press, 1993).

12. Frederick Engels, "Marx und die 'Neue Rheinische Zeitung' 1848–49," *Der Sozialdemokrat*, no. 11 (March 13, 1884). On the other hand, Marx is reported to have held Marat's *Chains of Slavery* in high esteem (Massin, *Marat*, 39).

13. *JRF* nos. 39 and 40, November 7 and 8, 1792.

# Index

References to materials in the notes include both the page number and note number and are italicized.

13/04/2025

14656489-0001